Collector's Guide to ANTIQUE CHOCOLATE MOLDS

with Values

by Wendy Mullen

Published by Hobby House Press, Inc.
Grantsville, Maryland
www.hobbyhouse.com

Angel on moon
unmarked
2½in (6cm) ca.1930.
Value $175

Front cover and title page: **Large bunny wearing apron** marked "Walters" #8560 — 20in (48cm) ca.1930. Value $1000.

Back cover: **Boy with toy horse** marked "Anton Reiche" #7531 — 6in (14cm) ca.1920; **Girl with doll** marked "Anton Reiche" #7532 — 6in (14cm)ca.1920. Value $350 for the pair. *Molds and Chalkware courtesy of Moni Marceau*

Sitting teddy bear marked "Anton Reiche" #24015 — 6in (14cm) ca.1920. Value $400. *Molded chocolate bear courtesy of The Chocolate Barn, photo by Christy Nevius.*

Additional copies of this book may be purchased at $29.95 (plus postage and handling) from
Hobby House Press, Inc.
1 Corporate Drive, Grantsville, MD 21536
1-800-554-1447
www.hobbyhouse.com
or from your favorite bookstore or dealer.

©2002 by Wendy Mullen

All rights reserved. No part of this book may be reproduced or utilized in any form or by any means, electronic or mechanical, including photocopying, recording, or by an information storage and retrieval system, without permission in writing from the publisher. Inquiries should be addressed to Hobby House Press, Inc., 1 Corporate Drive, Grantsville, MD 21536.

Printed in the United States of America

ISBN: 0-87588-618-3

Table of Contents

6 Chocolate and Chocolate Molds

8 Bunnies

32 Chicks

40 Animals

56 Halloween

60 People

88 Make-Believe

94 Clowns

98 Teddy Bears

102 Winter Fun

108 Christmas

136 Miscellaneous

140 Additional Information

Uncle Sam marked "Jaburg" #19
7in (16-½cm) ca.1900.
Value $800

Acknowledgements

I wish to thank God for giving me my dreams …… my husband for helping me fulfill my dreams…..and my friends and family for being part of my dreams!

Many thanks go to Moni Marceau—friends by a chance encounter, Frank Friedwald, Lucinda Gregory, Paul and Fredricka Schwanka, Rex Morgen, Lee and JoAnn Tripp, Rudi and Isabelle Nuyens, Susan Thompson—the great encourager, Ginny Betourne, Bruce, Lorry and Greg Hanes, my wonderful neighbor Diana Cassel, Barbara Bowers who is always there for me, the best prayer Debbie Dixon, and my sweet sisters Debbie and Brenda.

Boston Candy Store card.

Introduction

Welcome back in time to the whimsical world of molded chocolates, penny-candy and childhood memories. Molded chocolates in thousands of forms were extremely popular around the turn of the last century. With the Christmas holidays came the serious St. Nick chocolate figures, the jolly American Santas and the sincere Father Christmas'. Easter brought many styles of bunnies, eggs and chicks. Throughout the year, chocolates were available in many figures, such as animals, people, monuments and household items. The metal molds used to make these scrumptious memories are a highly prized collectible today. Molds that are in good condition with matching pieces without dents and rust are the recommended purchase, as well as those molds manufactured before WWII. The older German Santa molds are widely sought after by collectors as well as the wonderfully detailed bunnies in fantasy settings. A large percentage of chocolate molds are marked with either the manufacturers name and mold number or both. Those molds marked "Made in Germany" are usually older than those marked "Vormenfabriek" or "Made in Holland." Most collectors will agree that Anton Reiche, the German mold-maker was the master mold-maker, and his molds generally bring the higher prices. Many of his designs were copied by other mold-makers, which really was a compliment to his amazing artistic ability. The older German molds show a fantastic amount of detail and are wonderful for display, while the molds from Holland manufactured after the 1940's are less expensive and can easily be used for chocolate. In the amazing world of antique chocolate molds there really is something for everyone. Enjoy!

Boy and best friend
marked "Anton Reiche"
4in (10cm) ca.1920.
Value $175

Chocolate and Chocolate Molds

Columbus discovered America and chocolate! Actually not quite chocolate, but the cacao beans that would later be made into the chocolate that so many people love! The Aztecs enjoyed the drink made from the cacao beans — hot cocoa — for many years before Columbus took the beans back to Spain. About a hundred years later, hot cocoa was a highly sought after and prized drink for the upper class and later was widely available to everyone. Cocoa was advertised as nutritious, and as an elixir that was basically good for curing many medical conditions. It wasn't until the mid 1800's that the cacao beans were ground into chocolate for eating. The French Company of Letang Fils that had made molds for ice cream was the first company to manufacture molds for milk chocolate in 1832. The German companies of H. Walter in 1866 and Anton Reiche in 1870 soon followed suit. In the United States, during the late 1800's and early 1900's, the Eppelsheimer Company, Jaburg and The American Chocolate Mould Company began production of chocolate molds. The Anton Reiche company

Left: Cards depicting the process of making cocoa.

Right top: Trade card advertising chocolate.

Right bottom: Trade card advertising candy.

soon became the largest producer of metal chocolate molds in the world. From 1870 to about 1939, the firm made over 50,000 different designs for chocolate molds. The factory was so large that it had a train that ran between buildings. They had at least a thousand machines used for mold production and thousands of workers. Unfortunately, the factory was bombed during the war and lost nearly everything. Chocolate molds were made from tinned steel and during the war some companies used copper.

The processes involved to make a single design were quite complex. First, an artist would draw the desired object. Then it was sculpted out of plaster, which was cut in half and used to make a casting in sand. Finally, hot metal was poured into the sand and the front and back halves were formed, heat treated, and placed on a heavy press which stamped the design onto steel pieces by using 250 tons of pressure. The name of the manufacturer and a number was usually stamped into the steel for identification.

The American Chocolate Mould Company currently uses the original master dies to stamp out new chocolate molds. Sadly no other companies have survived the plastic age. There are only a few chocolatiers still using metal moulds for chocolate since plastic molds are widely available, cost less and are very easy to use. When a metal mold has rust or any loss of the tinning to the inside, the chocolate does not come out of the mold as easily or look quite as nice. The Chocolate Barn in Vermont still uses over 500 antique molds for making chocolate figures. A few examples are pictured in this book. Many antique mold designs have been made into plastic molds that are very detailed and easy to use. The Morgen Chocolate Company does use metal molds, but for production pieces, prefers plastic molds. Morgen Chocolate produces designs for plastic molds based on favorite antique molds and also designs new molds.

The subjects chosen for antique chocolate molds are absolutely incredible! Besides the Santas and bunnies most of us remember from childhood, there are animals, vehicles, people, fairy-tale and cartoon characters, statues, and holiday related items designed as chocolate molds. Many antique molds reflect the political views of that certain period, clothing styles and popular past times. Some molds were made to have a front and a back and were held together with clips. Others were hinged together in groups of two or more for the convenience of the chocolatiers who would be using them, while other designs were made to be single sided and were soldered together into flat chocolate molds. Antique molds are now being used for making candles, papier-mâché and chalkware. Metal chocolate molds can be cleaned by wiping with a damp cloth and then drying in a warm oven. Lee and JoAnn Tripp, who collect and sell antique chocolate molds at the website: *www.antiquemongers.com*, recommend soaking rusty molds for a day or two in a solution of vinegar, salt and hot water. When the mold is completely dry, rust can be removed by using a dremmel tool and very fine steel wool that won't scratch the mold surface. To prevent further rusting, an agent such as WD-40 can be applied. The mold will be clean but no longer suitable for chocolate molding. Since chocolate molds can be found at flea markets, antique stores and auctions, the pricing will vary quite a bit. This book will give realistic pricing for molds based on antique store values, not those realized at auctions or flea markets.

~Bunnies~

Left: Page from the Anton Reiche catalog showing chocolate mold designs. ca.1920

Bunny on motorcycle marked "Et Metro"
4-½in (10cm) ca.1930.
Value $85

Front and back view of **Egg house** marked "Anton Reiche"
#24227 — 4in (9cm) ca.1920.
Value $165

9

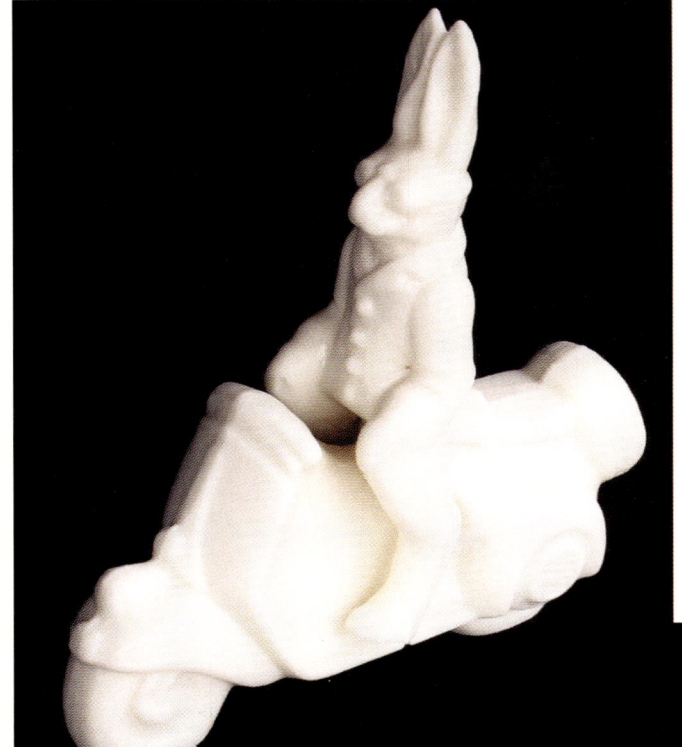

Above: **Bunny driving car** marked "Heris" #4157 7in (16-½cm) ca.1950.
Value $95

Left: White Chocolate-molded **Bunny riding motor scooter.**

Below: **Bunny rider and motor scooter:** bunny mold is 5-½in (13cm) and motor scooter is 6-½in (15-½cm) ca.1930. *Chocolate figures courtesy of The Chocolate Barn, photo by Christy Nevius.*
Value $295

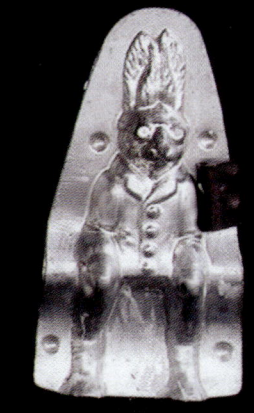

10

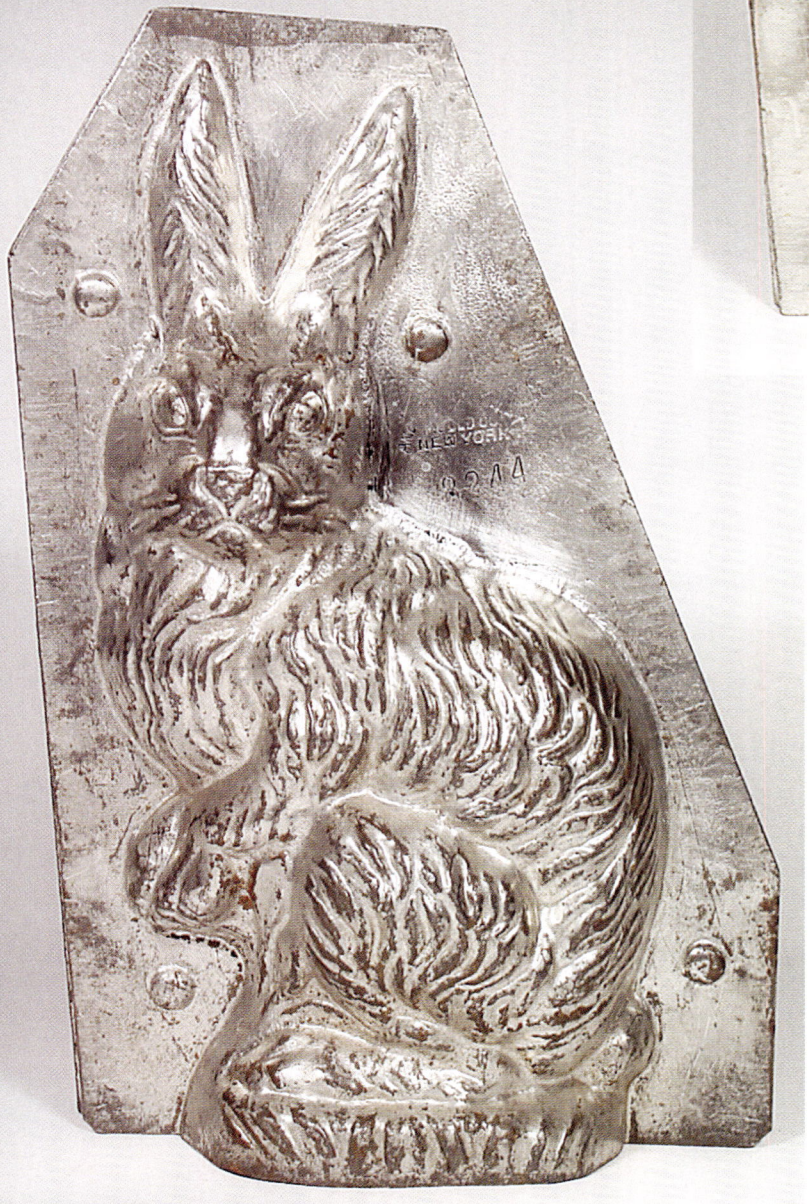

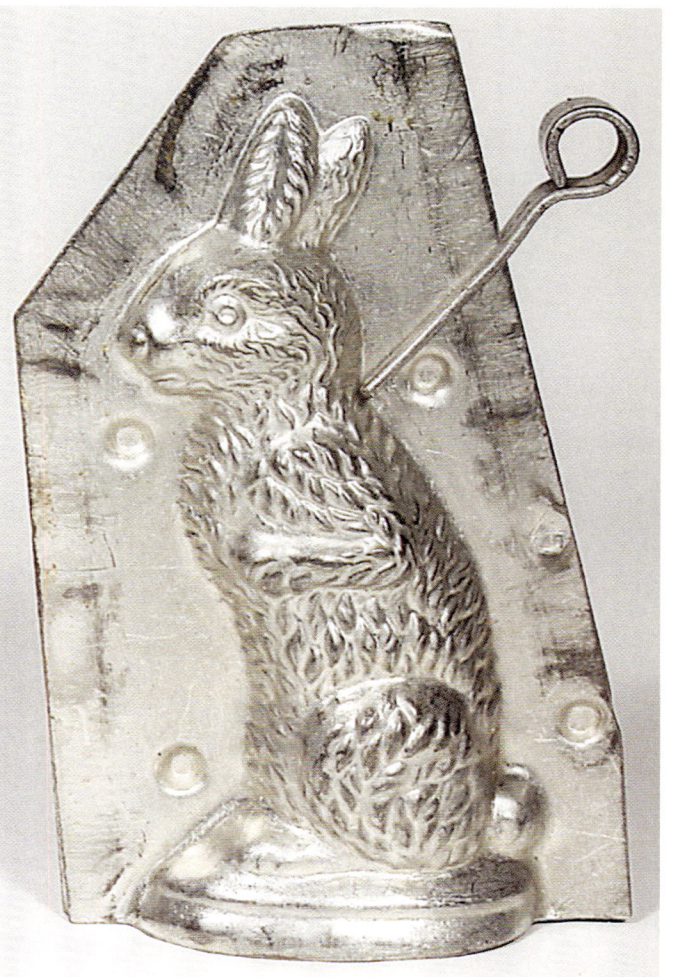

Small bunny marked "Jaburg" #4
5in (11-½cm) ca.1920.
Value $85

Startled bunny marked "American Chocolate Mould Co." #8244 — 10in (24cm) ca.1930.
Value $175

11

Piggyback bunnies marked "Anton Reiche" #6234 6-¼in (15cm) ca.1900. *Mold from the collection of Moni Marceau and Chalkware by Moni Marceau.* Value $225

Right: Page from the Anton Reiche catalog showing chocolate mold designs. ca.1920

Below: **Bunny with basket** marked "Eppelsheimer" #6218 — 12in (29cm) ca.1920. Value $150

12

Left: **Large Bunny wearing vest** marked "DeSmedt" #3152 — 20in (48cm) ca.1950. Value $295

Below: Postcard showing the similarity between chocolate mold designs and art.

13

Above: **Girl with bunny**
5in (11-½cm) ca.1930.
Value $95

Left: **Bunny with children**
5in (11-½cm) ca.1920.
Value $275

Left: **Bunny riding rooster** #443
5-½in (13cm) ca.1950.
Value $165

Below: **Musical bunnies: Bunny with sax**
4-½in (10-¼cm) ca.1950.
Value $65
Bunny with banjo marked "Anton Reiche"
#26023 — 6-½in (15-½cm) ca.1920.
Value $165
Bunny with accordion marked
"Riecke" — 5in (11-½cm) ca.1950.
Value $65

15

Left: Bunny with rifle marked "Eppelsheimer" #8038
5in (11-½cm) ca.1930.
Value $65

Right: **"Shooting" bunny** marked "Letang" #4055
4-½in (10-¼cm) ca.1930.
Value $65

16

Below: **Four classic bunnies:**
Left marked "Walters" #5316
4-½in (10-¼cm) ca.1935.
Value $95
Left Center #4174
4in (9cm) ca.1920.
Value $95
Right Center marked "Eppelsheimer"
#4602 — 7-½in (18cm) ca.1920.
Value $95
Right marked "Walters" #8683
5in (11cm) ca.1920.
Value $85

17

Mother bunny with baby marked
"Anton Reiche" #31779
8in (19cm) ca.1930.
Value $165

Small mother bunny holding baby
marked "Anton Reiche" — 3in (6-½cm)
ca.1910. *Collection of Moni Marceau.*
Value $225

Right: **Bride bunny** 7in (16-½cm) ca.1930.
Value $150

Middle: **Large running bunny** marked "Thos. Mills"
11in (27cm) ca.1910.
Value $175

Bottom: **Small dressed bunny riding bunny** marked
"Anton Reiche" #6404 — 4in (9cm) ca.1920.
*Chalkware by Moni Marceau,
mold from the collection of Moni Marceau.*
Value $225

19

Above: Page from the Anton Reiche catalog. ca.1920

Left: **Bunny pulling egg cart** marked "Et Metro" 4in (9cm) ca.1940. Value $65

Gnome riding bunny marked
"Jaburg" #34
5in (11-½cm) ca.1930.
Value $450

Small running bunny marked
"Anton Reiche" #6274
6in (14cm) ca.1920.
Value $145

Right: **Bavarian dress mother and son bunny** marked "Anton Reiche" 3in (6-½cm) ca.1920.
Collection of Moni Marceau.
Value $225

Below left: **Bavarian dressed lady bunny** marked "Walters" #4640 — 7in (16-½cm) ca.1920
Value $150

Below right: **Bavarian dressed male bunny** marked "Walters" #4639 — 7in (16-½cm) ca.1920
Value $150

22

Right: **Large bunny wearing apron** marked "Walters" #8560 20in (48cm) ca.1930. Value $1000

Left: **Bunny sitting on stump** 10in (24cm) ca.1930. Value $95

23

Easter Goods

PENNY CHOCOLATE EASTER NOVELTIES

Chocolate Marshmallow Rabbit—White marshmallow centers, chocolate covered.
2Y9581—120 in box....Box, **80c**

Chocolate Cream Pigs—Solid, chocolate coated.
2Y1134—120 in box....Box, **84c**

PENNY EASTER CANDY NOVELTIES

Asstd. Novelties—Decorated soft marshmallow rabbits, chicks, lambs and eggs. Asstd. colors.
2Y1046—100 in box....Box, **72c**

Rabbit—Soft, white marshmallow rabbits, sugared, with pink candy eyes.
2Y1152—120 in box....Box, **85c**

Chick—Soft yellow marshmallow chicks, sugared, colored candy eyes and bill.
2Y1153—120 in box....Box, **86c**

RABBIT SUCKERS

Penny Suckers—Asstd. flavors and colors, chewy hard candy on stick. Very attractive.
2Y1133—120 in box.....Box, **84c**

5c Suckers—Asstd. flavors and colors, chewy hard candy on stick. Very attractive.
2Y1135—24 in box......Box, **84c**

DECORATED MARSHMALLOW EASTER NOVELTIES

Asstd. Novelties—Large soft marshmallow pieces, decorated with sugar icing and colored sugar sand. Chicks, rabbits, eggs and lambs, asstd. in partitioned box.
2Y1047—24 in box......Box, **79c**

Nest Decoration—White marshmallow egg, decorated with colored sugar icing, nest with 3 red imperial eggs.
2Y1149—24 in box.,....Box, **89c**

5c CHOCOLATE EASTER NOVELTIES

5c Chocolate Coated Giant Marshmallow Rabbit—Marshmallow center, extra large sizes.
2Y1136—24 in box. Box, **87c**

5c Chicken on Nest—Vanilla cream center, chocolate covered, a 5c seller.
2Y9583—24 in box......Box, **87c**

5c Pig—Vanilla cream center, chocolate covered, a 5c seller.
2Y9584—24 in box......Box, **87c**

5c Chocolate Cream Egg—Good size fancy decorated icing, chocolate coated.
2Y1140—24 in box......Box, **90c**

5c Chocolate Cross—3¾ in., vanilla cream center, chocolate coated.
2Y1137—24 in box......Box, **90c**

5c Sitting Rabbit—Hollow molded cream, chocolate covered.
2Y1107—24 in box......Box, **90c**

5c Rooster—Hollow molded cream, chocolate covered.
2Y1108—24 in box......Box, **90c**

5c Wheelbarrow Chocolate Rabbit—Vanilla cream center, chocolate coated, very attractive.
2Y1139—24 in box......Box, **90c**

CHOCOLATE COATED CANDY EGGS

5c Sellers

Marshmallow Center—Double cast, pink and white chocolate covered.
2Y1312—24 in box......Box, **85c**

Cream Center—Asstd. flavors, cherry fruit, nut and vanilla flavors, dipped in chocolate, wt. about 2 oz. each.
2Y9325—24 in box......Box, **85c**

10c CHOCOLATE EASTER NOVELTIES

10c Sitting Rabbit—Hollow, molded cream, chocolate covered, decorated with sugar icing.
2Y1109—12 in box......Box, **90c**

10c Rooster—Hollow, molded cream chocolate covered, decorated with sugar icing.
2Y1110—12 in box......Box, **90c**

10c Chocolate Cross—5 in., vanilla cream center, chocolate coated.
2Y1138—12 in box.

Advertisement for chocolate bunnies. ca.1900

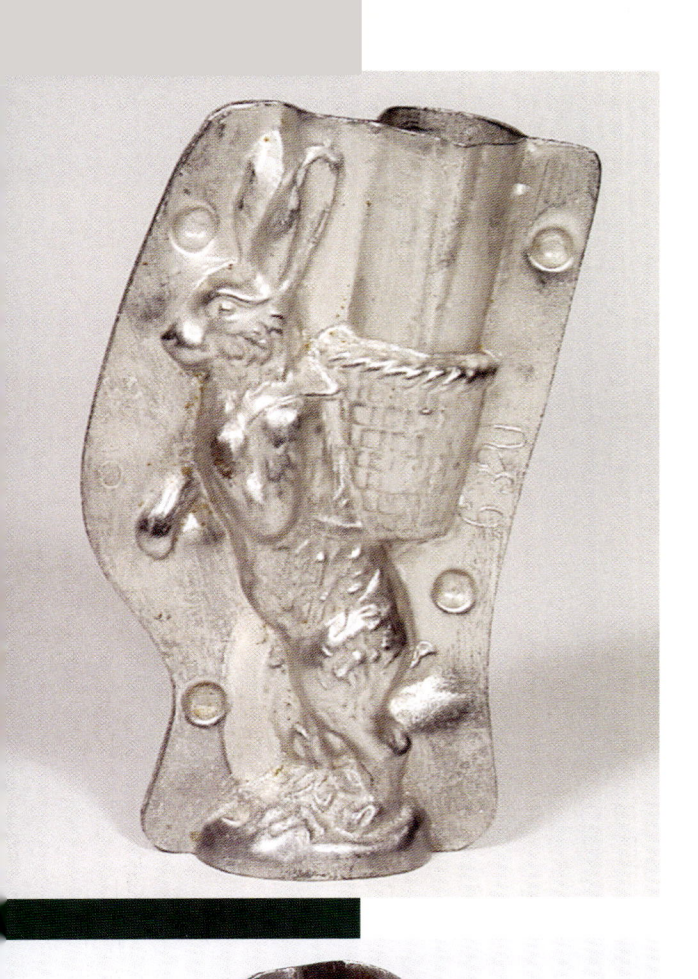

Left: **Small bunny carrying basket** marked "Anton Reiche" #6320 — 5in (11-¼cm) ca.1920. Value $125

Above: **Bunny sitting on basket of eggs** marked Laurosch #3050 — 6in (14cm) 1939. Value $65

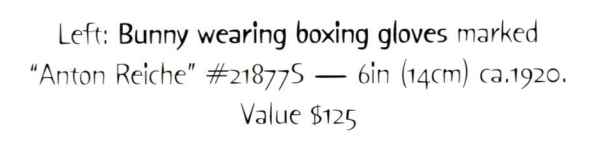

Left: **Bunny wearing boxing gloves** marked "Anton Reiche" #21877S — 6in (14cm) ca.1920. Value $125

Left: **Vendor bunny** marked "Anton Reiche" #16529 — 4-½in (10cm) ca.1920. Value $165

Opposite page, top: Page from the Anton Reiche catalog. ca. 1920

Opposite page, bottom: **Postcard mold of bunnies painting eggs** marked "Anton Reiche" #6695 7in (16cm) ca.1910. *Collection of Moni Marceau.* Value $395

Above: Wilbur coupon for a free candy bar. ca.1920

Right: **Small bunny with basket** marked "Anton Reiche" #6761 — 4-½in (10cm) ca.1920. Value $75
Bunny with walking stick marked "Riecke" #4011 — 7in (16cm) ca.1930. Value $65

26

Moules doubles.   Moldes para Chocolate.   Doppel-Formen für Chocolade.   Double moulds.

Nr. 6385. 90 Gramm.
Nr. 6386. 13 Gramm.
Nr. 6387. 100 Gramm.
Nr. 6388. 102 Gramm.
Nr. 6389. 70 Gramm.
Nr. 6390. 48 Gramm.
Nr. 6391. 11 Gramm.
Nr. 6395. 26 Gramm.
Nr. 6396. 26 Gramm.
Nr. 6397. 48 Gramm.
Nr. 6392. 31 Gramm.
Nr. 6393. 16 Gramm.
Nr. 6394. 10 Gramm.

Anton Reiche, Dresden.

24

27

Bunny pushing egg cart marked
"Anton Reiche" #6390
4in (9cm) ca.1920.
Value $95

Above: **Tall hiking bunny** #3164 — 16-½in (40cm) ca.1950.
Value $195

Left: Cover of the Saturday Evening Post from March 25, 1950, shows large chocolate bunnies being made.

29

Father bunny and son riding motorcycle
marked "Jos Boyen" #16106
5in (11cm) ca.1960.
Value $95

A Happy Eastertide

30

Left: **Bunny riding chick** marked "Heris" #4102 — 5-½in (13cm) 1950. Value $145

Below: **Three bunnies with no fur detail:** Sizes are 13in (31cm); 11in (27cm); and 6in (14cm) ca.1920. Values $175; $125; and $75 respectively

~Chicks~

Left: Page from the Anton Reiche catalog, ca.1920

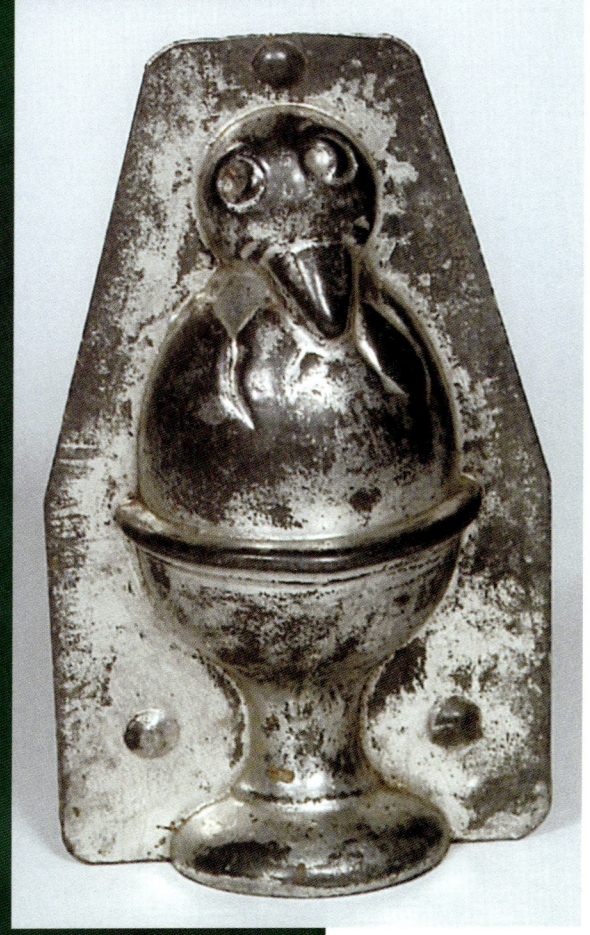

Above: **Chick hatching from egg** 3in (6cm) ca.1910.
Value $75

Left: **Chick in eggcup** marked "Letang" #4324
4-½in (10cm) ca.1900.
Value $75

Boy sitting on egg with
bunny hatching #5580
4-½in (10cm) ca.1930.
Value $125
Boy sitting on egg with chicks #5579
4-½in (10cm) ca.1930.
Value $125

Above: **Chicken pulling egg cart**
marked "Walters" #8427
4-½in (10cm) ca.1930.
Value $75

Right: **Three ducks** marked "Walters"
3in (6cm) ca.1920.
Value $75

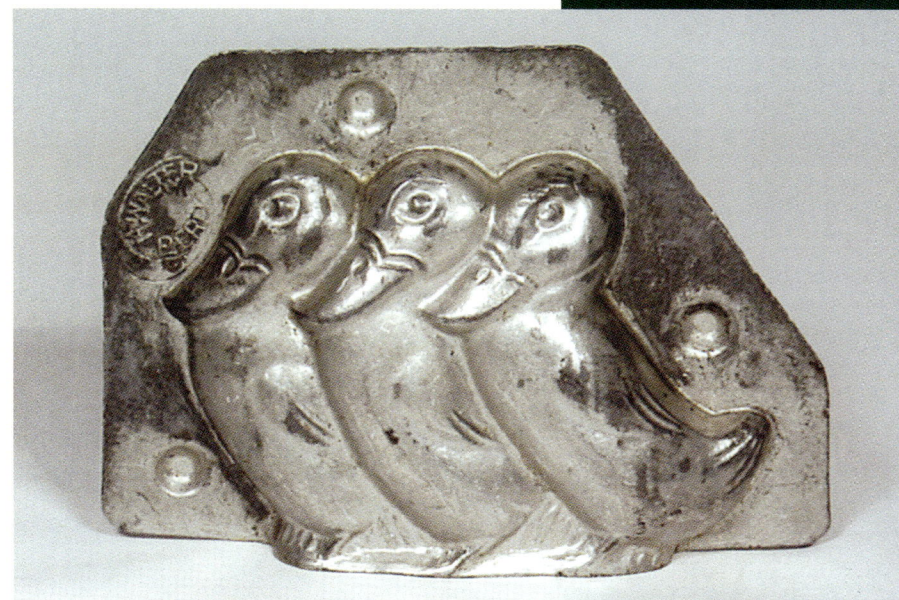

Chick pulling cart #28159
8in (19cm) ca.1920.
Value $125

Duck 4in (9cm) ca. 1920. *Chocolate duck by The Chocolate Barn, mold from collection of Lucinda Gregory, photo by Christy Nevius.*
Value $75

35

Rooster and chicken friends
marked "Eppelsheimer" #4809
3-½in (8cm) ca.1920.
Value $75

Above: **Small chick pulling cart**
marked "Anton Reiche" #26258
5in (11cm) ca.1900.
Value $75

Left: **Rooster hatching from egg**
5-½in (13cm) ca.1960.
Value $50

Big rooster marked
"Sommet" #1412
9-¾in (23-½cm)
ca.1900.
Value $175

Roosters: *Left* #5053 — 4in (9cm) ca.1920.
Value $75
Center marked "Anton Reiche" #24810 — 5-¾in (13-½cm) ca.1930.
Value $95
Right 3-½in (8cm) ca.1920.
Value $75

Chickens:
Left 5-½in (13cm) ca.1930.
Value $65
Left Center marked "Anton Reiche" #6698 4-½ in (10-½cm) ca.1920.
Value $75
Right Center 2in (4cm) ca.1920.
Value $45
Right 3-½in (8cm) ca.1910.
Value $75

~Animals~

Above: Advertising postcard for Hawley & Hoops candy showing molded chocolates.

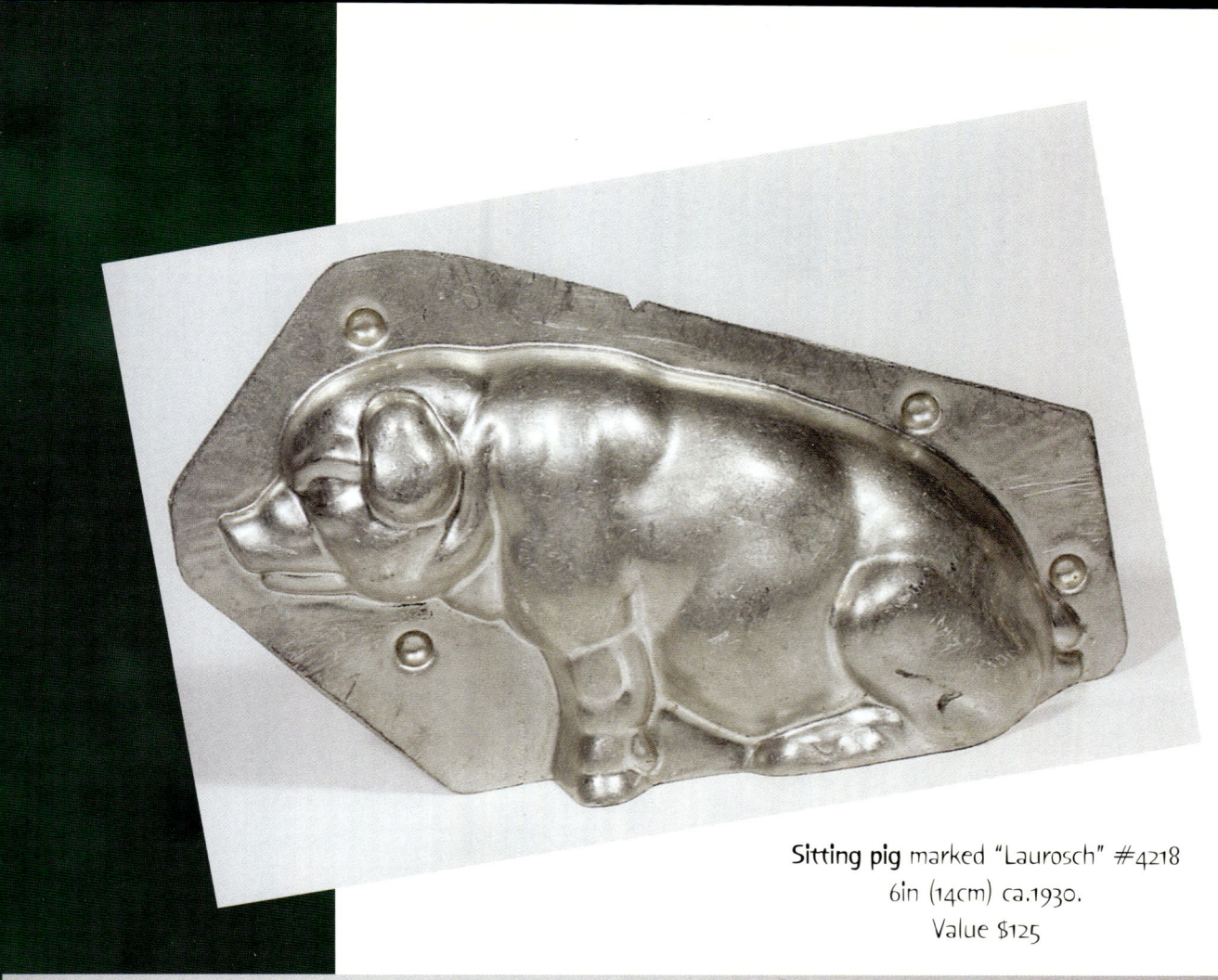

Sitting pig marked "Laurosch" #4218
6in (14cm) ca.1930.
Value $125

Swan with open back 5in (11-½cm) ca.1950.
Value $40
Swan with basket marked "Et Metro" 5-½in (13cm) ca.1950.
Value $65

41

Lamb marked "Laurosch" #4205
7in (17cm) ca.1930.
Value $95

Right: **Rhinoceros** marked "Anton Reiche #25466
7in (17cm) ca.1900.
Value $175

Below: **Animal Musicians flat mold** marked "Anton Reiche" #24079 — 7-½in (18cm) ca.1930. Molded chocolate musicians courtesy of The Chocolate Barn, photo by Christy Nevius.
Value $85

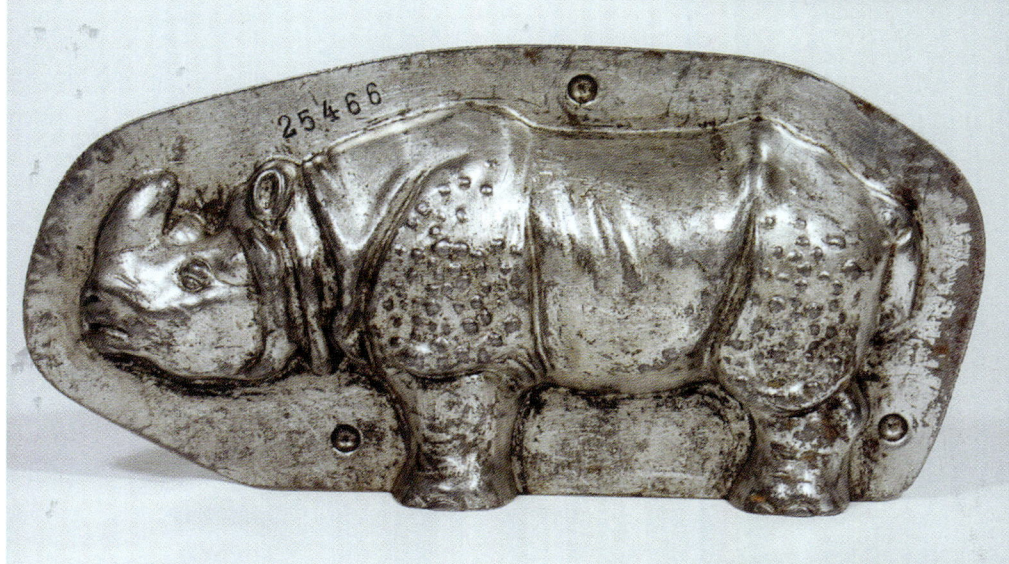

42

Standing elephant
11in (27cm) ca.1910.
Value $175

Elephants: *(left to right)*
6in (14cm) ca.1930. Value $65
3in (6-½cm) ca.1950. Value $40
6in (14cm) marked "Anton Reiche" #8303, ca.1900. Value $85
6in (14cm) ca.1920. Value $75
7in (16-½cm) ca.1920. Value $75
4in (9cm) #8307, ca.1920. Value $65

Gorilla #4067
6-½in (15-½cm) ca.1920.
Value $145

Monkey holding watermelon
marked "Walters" #8626
5in (11-½cm) ca.1930.
Value $95

Monkey on scooter
marked
"Walters" #8675
4in (9cm) ca.1930.
Value $95

Wild boar marked "Sommet"
7-½in (18cm) ca.1920.
Value $125

Donkey marked "Sommet"
5in (12cm) ca.1920.
Value $95

45

Hippopotamus
4in (9cm) ca.1920.
Value $125

Camel marked
"Letang" #3641
5in (11-½cm) ca.1920.
Value $95

Three bears:
Left 4-½in (10-½cm)
marked "Eppelsheimer"
#4800, ca.1920.
Value $65
Center 6-½in (15-½cm)
#5721, ca.1900.
Value $95
Right 5in (12cm) marked
"Letang" #3630, ca.1930.
Value $75

Above: **Lion**
4in (9cm) ca.1930.
Value $65

Left: **Lion**
marked "Sommet"
6in (14cm) ca.1920.
Value $95

47

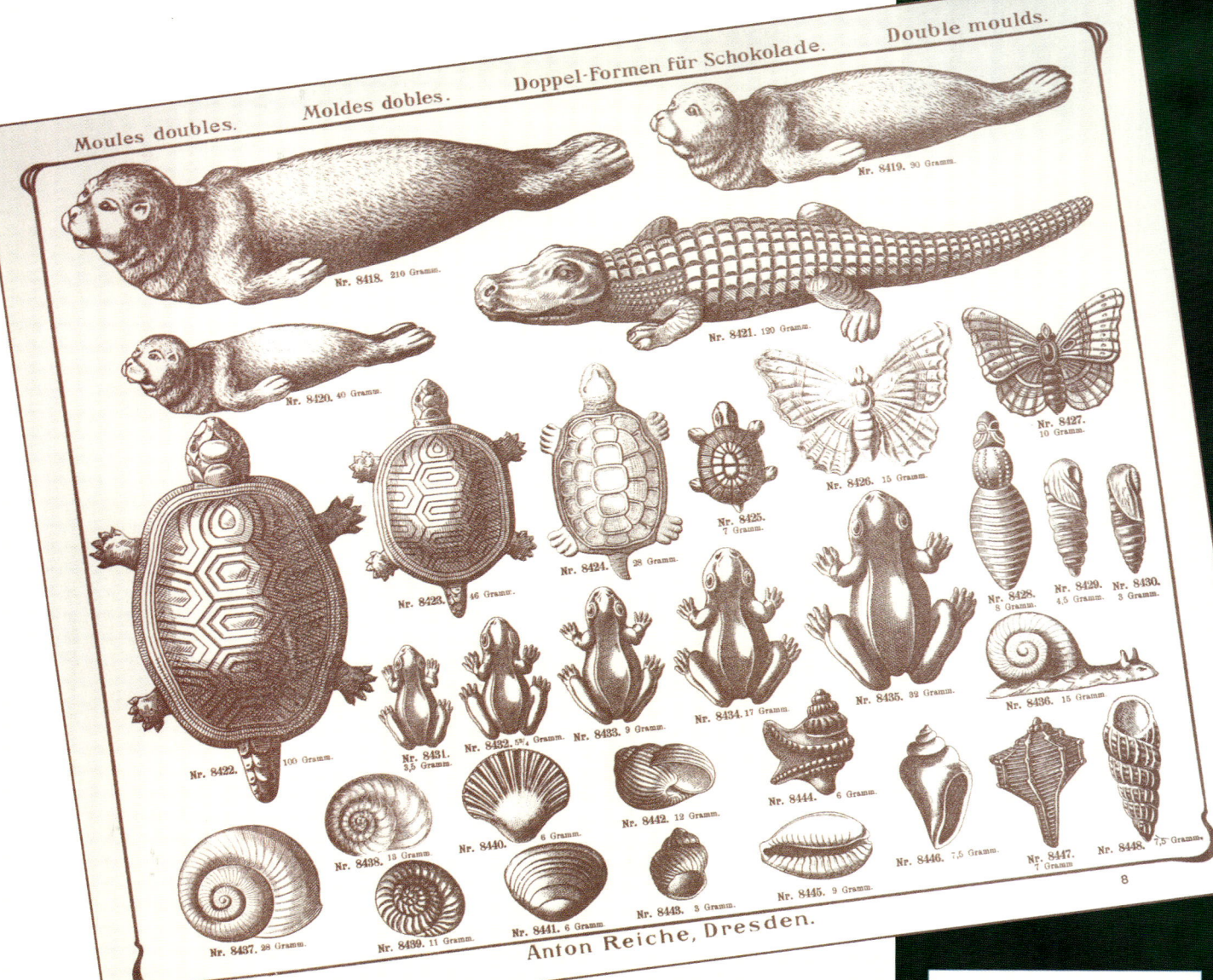

Above: Page from the Anton Reiche catalog. ca.1920

Left: **Alligator** 9in (21-½cm) ca.1900. Value $175

48

Penguins
Left #5902
4-½in (10-½cm) ca.1900.
Value $95.
Right marked "Letang" #4970
4-½in (10-½cm) ca.1930.
Value $65

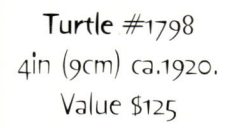

Turtle #1798
4in (9cm) ca.1920.
Value $125

Fish: *Left* 10in (24cm) ca.1900.
Value $95
Right 12in (29cm) ca.1900.
Value $95

Big fish marked "Anton Reiche"
#20891S — 14in (34cm) ca.1900.
Collection of my son, Richie.
Value $175

49

Below: **Horse pulling cart** marked
"Anton Reiche" #30331
8in (19cm) ca.1920.
Value $195

50

Below: **Dog pulling cart with milk bottles**
marked "Anton Reiche" #29342
10in (24cm) ca.1920.
Value $225

51

Left: **Bulldog** marked
"Walters" #8338
5in (11-½cm) ca.1920.
Value $125

Above: **Dogs:** *Left* #21044 — 5-½in (13cm) ca.1920.
Value $85
Left Center #7371 — 3in (6cm) ca.1950.
Value $65
Right Center #13151 — 3-½in (8cm) ca.1920.
Value $95
Right marked "Made in Holland" 5-½in (13cm) ca.1950.
Value $65

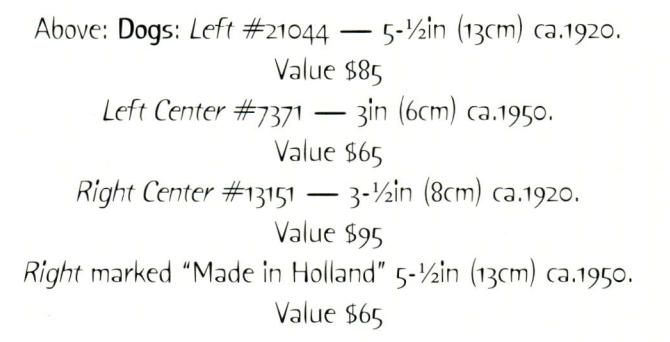

Right: **Poodle** marked "Sommet" #1306
9in (22cm) ca.1900.
Value $150

Left: **Beautiful pug dog**
#8650 — 5in (11-½cm)
ca. 1920.
Value $125

Below: Page from the Anton Reiche catalog.
ca. 1920

53

Right: **Large cat** marked "Anton Reiche" #865
5-½in (13cm) ca.1900.
Value $145
Smaller cat #8667
4-½in (10cm) ca.1900.
Value $95

Above: **Cat flat mold** marked "Riecke" #3317
7in (16-½cm) ca.1930.
Value $75

Right: **Cat and dog friends** 4in (9cm) ca.1950.
Value $75

Left: Cats playing banjos marked "Anton Reiche" #27621 6in (14cm) ca.1930. Value $125

Below: Ghirardelli's chocolate company coloring book giveaway. ca.1910

Compliments of *D. Ghirardelli Co.* San Francisco.

~Halloween~

Left: **Jack-o-lantern** marked "Eppelsheimer" #7400 — 3in (6cm) ca.1920.
Value $225

Above: **Rare four-piece mold of the "Spitten Kitten"** marked "Laurosch" #3058 7in (16-½cm) ca.1930. *Collection of Paul and Fredricka Schwanka.*
Value $395

Left: Wonderful papier-mâché form of "Spitten Kitten" by *Ginny Betourne of TroutCreekFolkArt.com.*

57

Right: **Hinged witch mold** marked "Anton Reiche" #25341 4in x 7in (9cm x 16-½cm) ca.1920. Value $250

Below: Original master dies for **witch chocolate** molds made by the American Chocolate Mould Co. *Collection of American Chocolate Mould Co.*

Below: Original master dies for **witch sucker** molds made by the American Chocolate Mould Co. *Collection of American Chocolate Mould Co.*

59

Chocolate trade card.

~People~

Girl riding scooter marked
"Anton Reiche" #30478
5in (12cm) ca.1920.
Value $125

Below:
Boy rowing boat marked
"Anton Reiche" #31901
5in (11-½cm) ca.1930.
Value $95
Boy riding tri-cycle marked
"Anton Reiche" #21472
5in (11-½cm) ca.1930.
Value $95
Boy driving car marked
"Anton Reiche" #32407
5-½in (13cm) ca.1930.
Value $95

61

Kids playing leapfrog marked
"Schwarzer" #2170
6in (14cm) ca.1930.
Value $95

Above: Cocoa trade card.

Left: **Boy with dog** marked "Anton Reiche"
#30337 — 8in (19cm) ca.1910.
Value $145

Left: **Crying boy** marked "Anton Reiche"
#22848 — 8in (19cm) ca.1920.
Value $145

Below: **Crying boy with dog** marked
"Walters" #8623 — 4in (9cm) ca.1920.
Value $125

63

Above: Page from the Anton Reiche catalog. ca.1920

Right: **Girl in swimsuit** marked "Anton Reiche" #2465 — 7in (16-½cm) ca.1920. Molded chocolate of the swimmer girl courtesy of *The Chocolate Barn*, photo by Christy Nevius. Value $175

Top left: **Girl dressed for costume party** marked "Anton Reiche" #17514 7in (16-½cm) ca.1920. Value $125

Top right: **Best-friends** marked "Anton Reiche" #7540 5in (11-½cm) ca.1920. Value $175

Left: Ghirardelli's coloring book. ca.1910

65

Far Left: Rare **Girl on swing** marked "Anton Reiche" #7889 4in (9cm) ca.1900. Value $175

Left: Back view of **Girl on swing**.

Below: Page from the Anton Reiche catalog. ca.1920

66

Boy riding goat marked
"Anton Reiche" # 8537
4in (9cm) ca.1920.
Collection of Moni Marceau.
Value $225

67

Above: **Charlie Chaplin** marked "Sommet" #4706
6in (14cm) ca.1920.
Value $95

Right: **Fountain boy** marked "Anton Reiche" #20452
5in (11-½cm) ca.1910.
Value $95

Above: **Olympians:**
Left 4-½in (10cm) ca.1920. Value $125
Center marked "Anton Reiche" #20756
5in (11-½cm) ca.1920. Value $125
Right marked "Anton Reiche" #20752
4-½in (10-½cm) ca.1920. Value $125

Soccer player #26069 — 8in (19cm) ca.1920.
Value $175

Football player #26694 — 5in (11-½cm) ca.1920.
Value $95.

69

Above: **Shy Susie** marked "Anton Reiche" #22607S — 6in (14cm) ca.1920. Value $150

Right: **Mary Janes: Holding cat** marked "Anton Reiche" #21220 7in (16-½cm) ca.1920. Value $125
Holding watering can marked "Anton Reiche" #21221 — 7in (16-½cm) ca.1920. Value $125

70

Girls: *Left* marked "Walters" #5285 — 6-½in (15-½cm) ca.1920.
Value $125
Center 8in (19cm) ca.1920.
Value $145
Right marked "Anton Reiche" #23007 — 6-½in (15-½cm) ca.1920.
Value $125

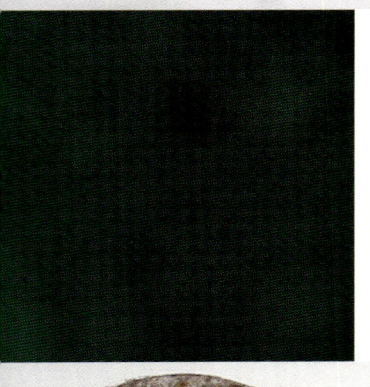

Above: **Polly on the pot** marked "Anton Reiche" #20533 — 6-½in (15-½cm) ca.1920.
Value $125

Left: **Kewpie doll** 7-½in (18cm) ca.1920.
Value $125
Dressed kewpie girl 5in (11-½cm) ca.1920.
Value $75

71

Right: Boy playing saxophone marked "Letang" #3889 6-½in (15-½cm) ca.1930.
Value $125

Sailor playing accordion marked "Reiche" #4039 3-½in (8cm) 1925. Chocolate sailor made by author and children using "Wilton candy melts."
Value $75

Hinged mold of boys playing accordions marked "Anton Reiche" #27699 6-½in x 3-½in (15-½cm x 8cm) ca.1920.
Value $95

72

Above: **Hinged mold of school boys** marked "Anton Reiche" 9in x 3-½in (22cm x 8cm) ca.1920. Value $125

73

Girl in night-gown
marked "Walters" #5291
6in (14cm) ca.1920.
Value $95

Dolls: *Left* #7809
4in (9cm) 1900.
Value $95
Right #7800
7-½in (18cm) ca.1900.
Value $125

Above: **Boys:** *(left to right)*
Tommy marked "Anton Reiche" #17502 — 5in (11-½cm) ca.1920. Value $45
Squatting boy #4059 — 4-½in (10-½cm) ca.1920. Value $65
Boy 3in (7cm) ca.1930. Value $45
Tough Tommy 6-¾in (16cm) ca.1930. Value $75
Boy marked "Anton Reiche" #24762 — 6in (14cm) ca.1920. Value $95
Tommy with ball #2103 — 5-½in (13cm) ca.1930. Value $95

Above: **Fisherman**
4-½in (10-½cm) ca.1920.
Value $55

Left: Old advertisement showing molded chocolate "Tots".

75

Left: **Bride and Groom** marked "Anton Reiche" #23344 (bride) and 23343 (groom) 7-½in (18cm) ca.1920. Value $295 for the pair

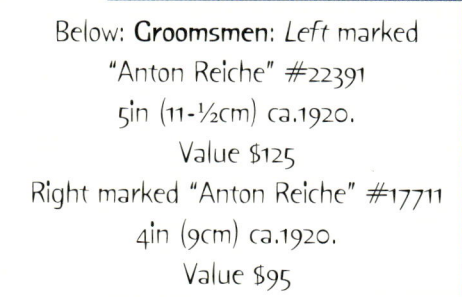

Below: **Groomsmen:** *Left* marked "Anton Reiche" #22391 5in (11-½cm) ca.1920. Value $125
Right marked "Anton Reiche" #17711 4in (9cm) ca.1920. Value $95

Left: Old die-cut Victorian children. ca.1900.

76

Above: **Art noveau ladies** marked
"Eppelsheimer" #4796
8in x 5in (19cm x 11-½cm) ca.1930.
Value $125

Left: **Railroad signal holder** marked
"Sommet" #2103
4-½in (10-½cm) ca. 1900.
Value $95
Poor friend #3697
4in (9cm) ca.1900.
Value $75

77

Right: **Puppy biting delivery boy**
marked "Letang" #3995
5-½in (13cm) ca.1920.
Value $150

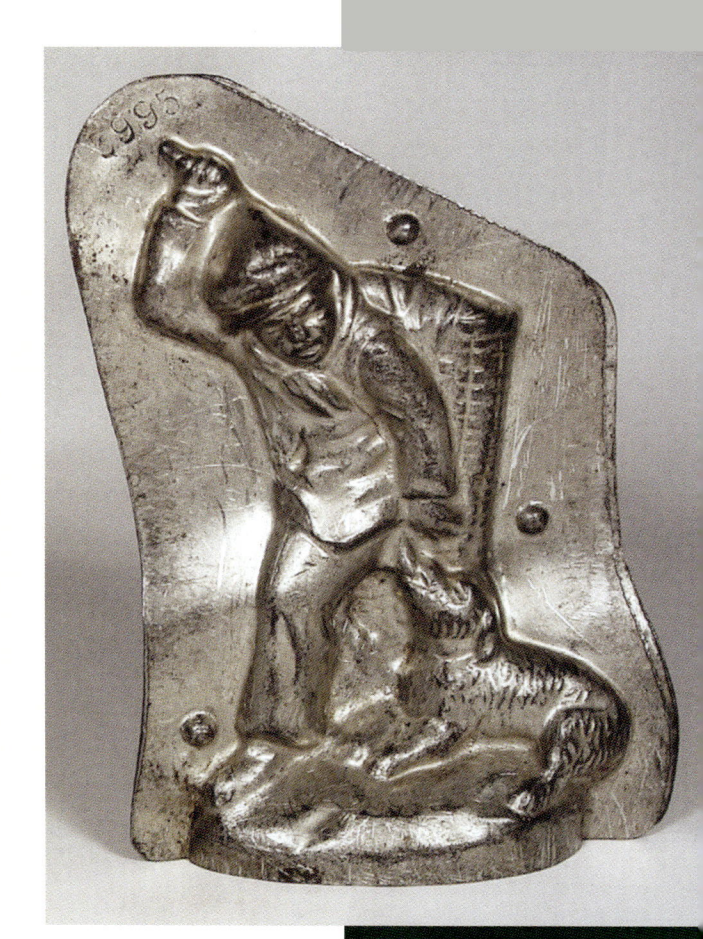

Right: **Dog biting little girl's doll** marked "Anton Reiche" #8610 —
4-½in (10-½cm) ca.1910.
Value $225

Left: **Fisher boy and girl** marked "Anton Reiche" #7544 (boy) and #7545 (girl) 5in (11-½cm) ca.1920.
Value $295 for the pair

Above: **Art deco style girl** marked "Anton Reiche" #26327 6in (14cm) ca.1930.
Value $150

Left: **Bellhop and friend** 6-½in (15-½cm) ca.1920.
Value $100 for the pair

79

Lady with umbrella marked "Anton Reiche" #26203
6in (14cm) ca.1920.
Value $150

Shy Dutch girl marked "Anton Reiche" #17605
6in (14cm) ca.1920.
Value $95

Old die-cut trade card for cocoa.

Left: **Tall policeman** marked "Anton Reiche" #21151
7in (16-½cm) ca.1920.
Value $125

Above: **O'Malley** marked "Anton Reiche" #15539
11in (26-½cm) ca.1920.
Value $175.

Left: **Traffic cop** marked "Walters" 4-½in (10-½cm ca.1920.
Value $75

81

Man riding bike
marked
"Sommet" #1519
9in (22cm) ca.1910.
Value $175

Big man on little bike
marked "Anton Reiche"
#25628
5in (11-½cm) ca. 1920.
Value $95

Men on bikes: *Left* marked "Sommet" 4in (9cm) ca.1920. Value $65
Right #517 — 4in (9cm) ca.1930. Value $65

Below left: **Lady with basket of apples** marked "Anton Reiche" #5283 5in (11-½cm) ca.1920. Value $150

Below right: **Baker man** 5in (11-½cm) ca.1930. Value $125

83

Man riding horse marked
"Sommet" #7811 — 9in (22cm)
ca.1910.
Value $175

Jockey marked "Anton Reiche"
#17540 — 5in (11-½cm) ca.1920.
Value $75

Cowboy riding horse 5in (11-½cm) ca.1930.
Value $75
Indian riding horse marked "Et Metro" 5in (11-½cm) ca.1930.
Value $75

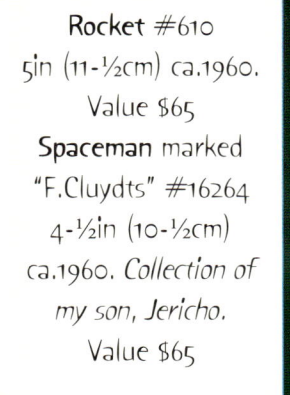

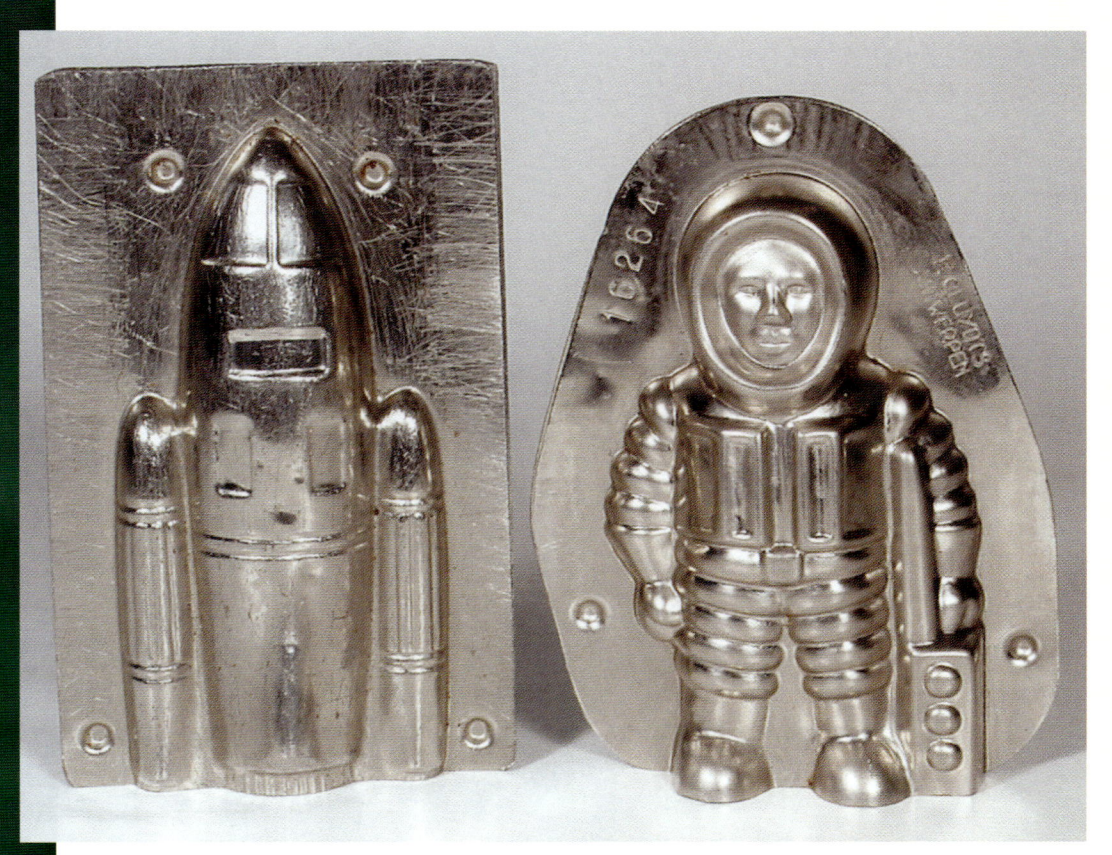

Rocket #610 5in (11-½cm) ca.1960.
Value $65
Spaceman marked "F.Cluydts" #16264 4-½in (10-½cm) ca.1960. Collection of my son, Jericho.
Value $65

85

Left: **Coal miner** marked "Anton Reiche" #14793 5in (11-½cm) ca.1920.
Value $150

Below: **Motorcycle with riders** marked "Anton Reiche" #1753 — 5in (11-½cm) ca.1920.
Value $165

Soccer player 4-½in (10-½cm) ca.1930.
Value $65
Tennis player 5in (11-½cm) ca.1930.
Value $65

86

Old print of the Statue of Liberty being built in Paris

Statue of Liberty marked "Anton Reiche" #21869
9-½in (23cm) ca.1920. Chocolate Statue of Liberty courtesy of
The Chocolate Barn, photo by Christy Nevius.
Value $800

STOLLWERCK'S EXHIBIT will be found conspicuous among the many noteworthy objects at the Worlds' Fair, in the shape of a Temple Renaissance style, of a height of 38 feet, composed entirely of Chocolate, 30,000 pounds, (supported by and covering a wooden frame), and Cocoa Butter, by an artistic application of the latter a marble effect is produced in many parts.

The prominent feature of this exhibit is a statue of Germania, 10 feet high, modeled after the celebrated "Niederwald" Monument, and sculptured out of a solid block of 2,200 pounds of Chocolate, the Pedestal being decorated with reliefs—more than life size—of the Emperors William I, Frederick III and William II, as well as of the Paladins, Bismarck and Moltke.

The structure rests upon a foundation formed by massive blocks of Chocolate, and above the Architrave the six columns are crowned by flying eagles of solid chocolate, while the dome is decorated with the Imperial Crown of Germany.

Stollwerck Bros., are purveyors to the courts of 26 European Sovereigns, and the firm employs over 2,000 hands. Stollwerck's Chocolates and Cocoas have been awarded 56 prize medals at different Exhibitions, and are for sale in all the leading Grocery and Confectionery stores.

Front and back of trade card advertising the Statue of Germania
displayed at the Columbian Exposition by Stollwercks 1893.

~Make Believe~

Left: Page from the Anton Reiche catalog. ca.1920

Disney's Donald Duck (made of copper during the war when steel was scarce) 6in (14cm) ca.1940.
Value $95

Felix the Cat marked "Anton Reiche" #13006
5in (11-½cm) ca.1930.
Value $175

Disney's Mickey Mouse marked "Vormenfabriek" #15266
7in (16-½cm) ca.1950.
Value $75

89

Above: **Warner Bros. Bugs Bunny** marked "Warner Bros."
7in (16-½cm) ca.1960. Value $150.

Right: **Wizard** #9964 — 5in (11-½cm) ca.1940.
Value $175

Below: **Fairy-tale characters:** *(left to right)*
Large gnome marked "Laurosch" #4466
7in (17cm) ca.1950. Value $95
Gingerbread house marked "Holland Handicrafts" #3697
6in (14cm) ca.1960. Value $50
Little Red Riding Hood 4in (9cm) ca.1960. Value $50
Gingerbread house marked "Vormenfabriek" #15374
5in (11-½cm) ca.1950. Value $95
Disney's Thumper 6-½in (15-½cm) ca.1950. Value $45
Pinocchio's cat Figueroa marked "Vormenfabriek" #16307
3-¾in (8-½cm) ca.1950. Value $45

Little Red Riding Hood and The Big Bad Wolf marked "Hornlein" #2596 6in (14cm) ca.1930.
Value $125

Little Red Riding Hood marked "Riecke" 7in (16-½cm) ca.1930. Chocolate Red Riding Hood and chocolate mold courtesy of The Chocolate Barn, photo by Christy Nevius.
Value $85

Little Red Riding Hood marked "Anton Reiche" #17454 — 6-½in (15-½cm) ca.1920.
Value $95

91

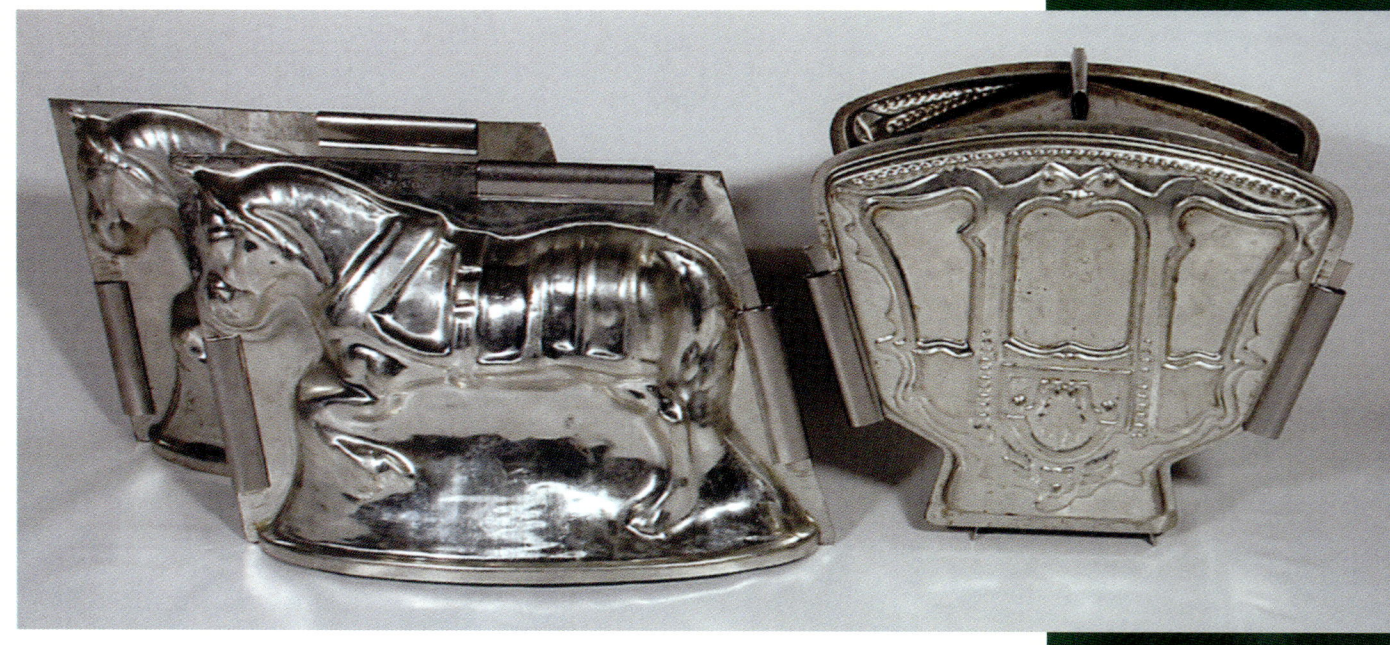

Above: **Cinderella's carriage and horses** marked "Christian" Carriage 7in (16-½cm); horses 10in (24cm) ca.1960.
Value $350

Left: **Genie** marked "Hans Bruhn" 5in (11-½cm) ca.1950.
Value $75

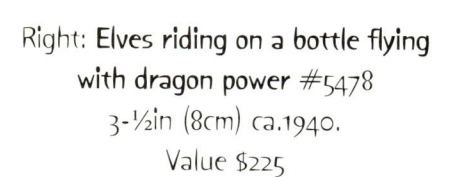

Right: **Elves riding on a bottle flying with dragon power** #5478 3-½in (8cm) ca.1940.
Value $225

Above: **Rocking horse** marked "Hans Bruhn" 5in (11-½cm) ca.1940.
Value $65

Puss 'n boots marked "Vormenfabriek"
#16310 — 4-½in (10-½cm) ca.1960.
Value $125

Daniel Boone marked "American Chocolate
Mould Co." 5-¼in (12-½cm) ca.1960.
Value $65

93

~Clowns~

Front, inside and back view of **Hinged mold with two boys dressed as clowns** marked "Anton Reiche" 16in (38cm) ca.1920.
Value $250

White chocolate molded clowns- *courtesy of The Chocolate Barn, photo by Christy Nevius.*

95

Above: **Boy dressed as clown with heart** marked "Anton Reiche" #24716 — 6in (14cm) ca.1920.
Mold from collection of Susan Thompson.
Value $200

Above right: **Clown holding rose** marked "Letang" #3720 — 8in (19cm) ca.1920.
Value $175

Right: **Boy dressed as a clown pointing to moon** marked "Letang" #3915 — 7in (16-½cm) ca.1930.
Mold from the collection of Moni Marceau, and Chalkware by Moni Marceau.
Value $150

Baby sitting on the world marked
"Walters" #8565
4-½in (10-½cm) ca.1920.
Value $125

Clown sitting on the world marked
"Walters" #8564
4-½in (10-½cm) ca.1920.
Value $125

Big clown with little hat marked "Anton Reiche" #15537 — 10in (24cm) ca.1910.
Value $175

Clown marked "Letang" #3704 — 8in (19cm) ca.1950.
Chocolate mold and molded chocolate courtesy of Lucinda Gregory at The Chocolate Barn, photo by Christy Nevius.
Value $95

97

~Teddy Bears~

Above: Page from the Anton Reiche catalog, ca.1920

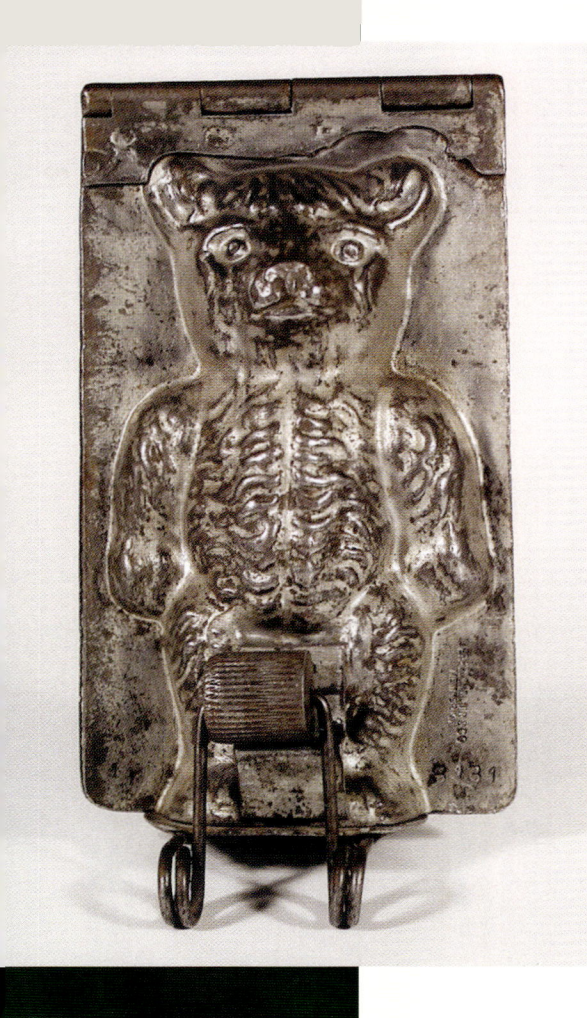

Left: **Hinged standing teddy bear** marked "Eppelsheimer" 5in (11-½cm) ca.1920. Value $175

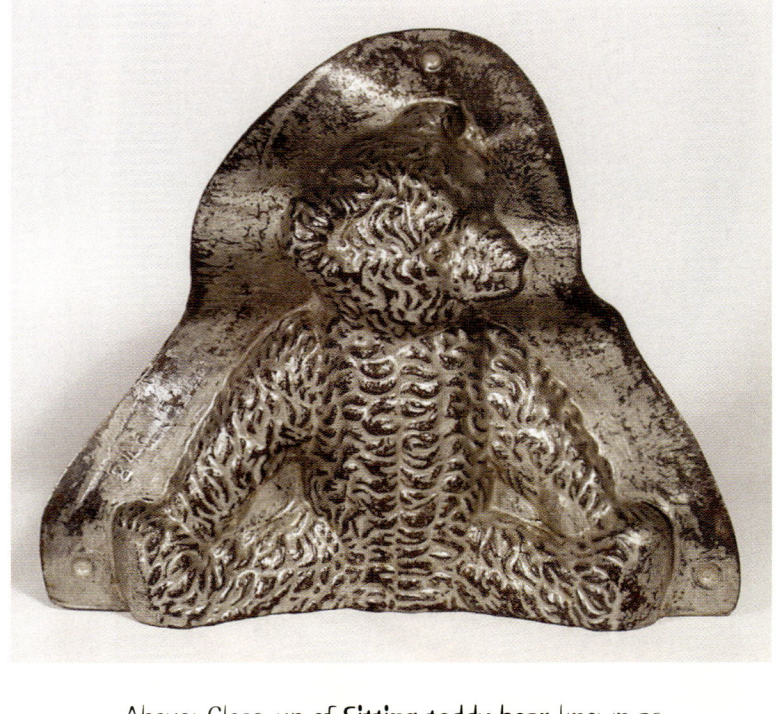

Above: Close-up of **Sitting teddy bear** known as "Cocoa Bear".

Left: **Teddy bear dancing with little boy** #13149 4in (9cm) ca.1920. *Collection of Moni Marceau.* Value $295

99

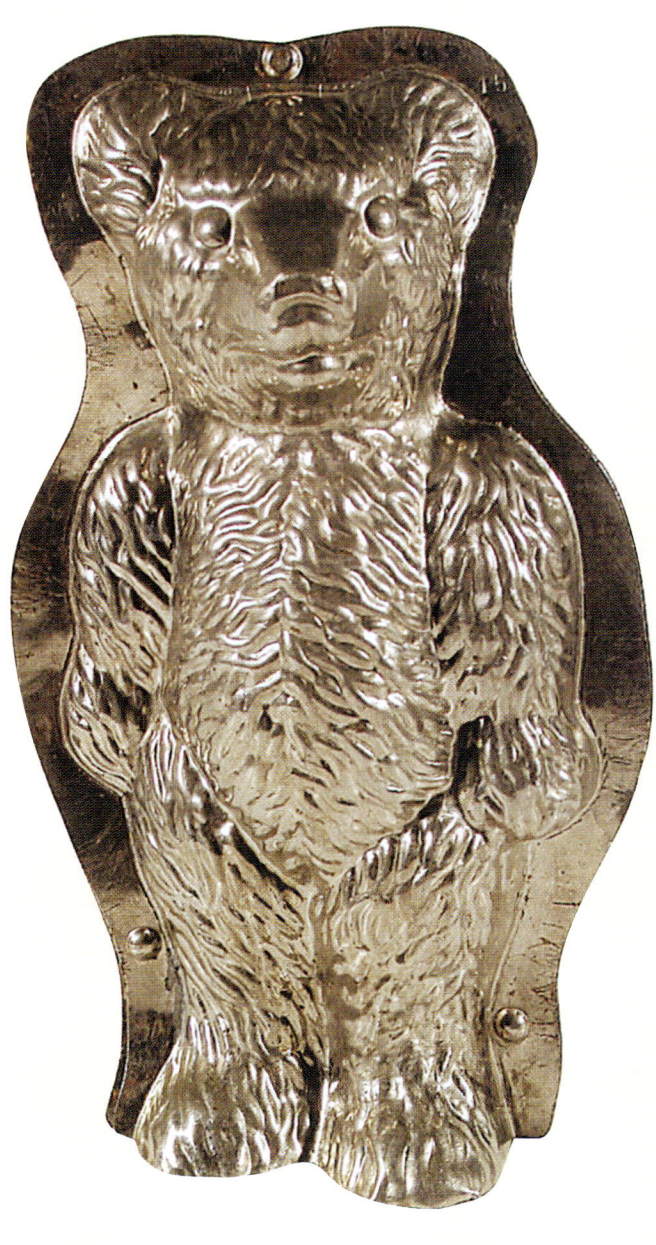

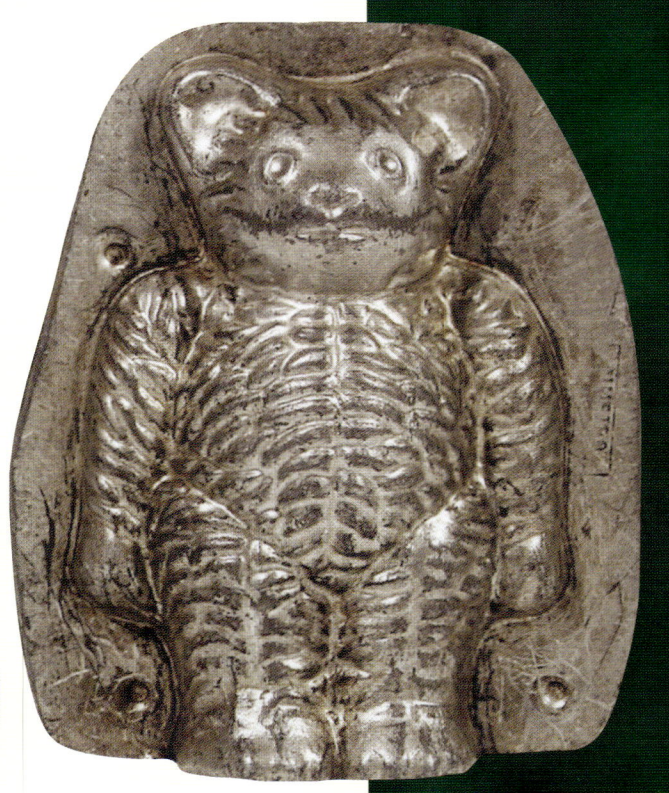

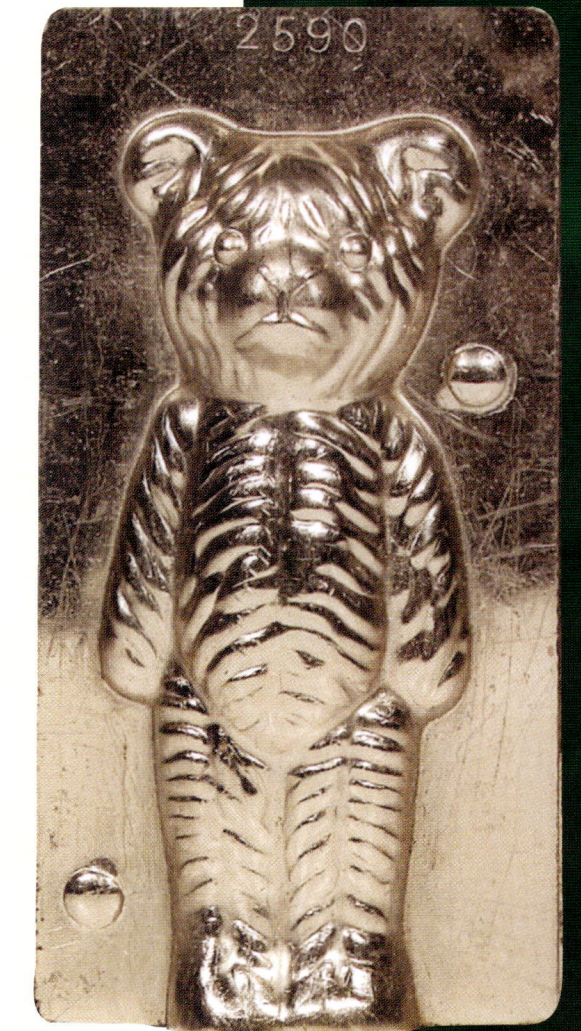

Above left: **Big standing teddy bear** #15 11in (27cm) ca.1940.
Value $350

Above right: **Cat-faced teddy bear** marked "Et Metro"
5in (11-½cm) ca.1930.
Value $75

Right: **Skinny teddy bear** #2590 — 5in (11-½cm) ca.1950.
Value $65

Above: **Standing teddy bear** #25885 6in (14cm) ca.1920. Mold from collection of Moni Marceau and Chalkware by Moni Marceau.
Value $275

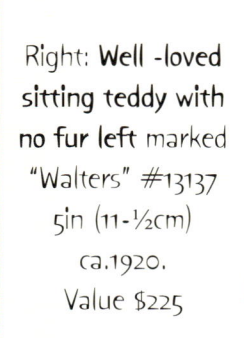

Right: **Well-loved sitting teddy with no fur left** marked "Walters" #13137 5in (11-½cm) ca.1920.
Value $225

101

~Winter Fun~

Left: Page from the Anton Reiche catalog. ca.1920

Front, back and side view of a rare **three-piece mold of three children riding on a sled** marked "Anton Reiche" #16731 — 5in (11-½cm) ca.1920. *Collection of Moni Marceau.* Value $395

103

Boy on sled marked "Letang" #4632 — 6in (14cm) ca.1930. Value $125

104

Above left: **Small girl on sled** marked "Anton Reiche" #7328 — 3in (6-½cm) ca.1910.
Value $175

Above right: **Girl made for sled** marked "Anton Reiche" #14795 — 5-½in (13cm) ca.1910. This mold went with a wooden sled purchased as an accessory shown on the Anton Reiche catalogue page (see page 102).
Value $175

Left: **Flat chocolate mold with cherubs** marked "Anton Reiche" #5175 — 9in (22cm) ca.1920.
Value $125

Left: **Angel** #13053
5in (11-½cm) ca.1920.
Value $225

Below: Page from the Anton Reiche catalog. ca.1920

106

Left: **Snowman** marked "Walters" #8104
5in (11-½in) ca.1920.
Value $295

Below: **Snowman** marked "Vormenfabriek"
7in (16-½cm) ca.1950. *White chocolate snowman by author and family using candy melts.*
Value $85

107

This "turn-of-the-century" postcard appeared in *Santa Claus Perforated Postcards* book published by the Merrimack Publishing Corp.

A Merry Christmas

~Christmas~

Front and side view of rare **three-piece Santa with bag** marked "Laurosch" #30326 6in (14cm) ca.1920. Collection of Paul and Fredricka Schwanka. Value $350.

This "turn-of-the-century" postcard appeared in *Santa Claus Perforated Postcards* book published by the Merrimack Publishing Corp.

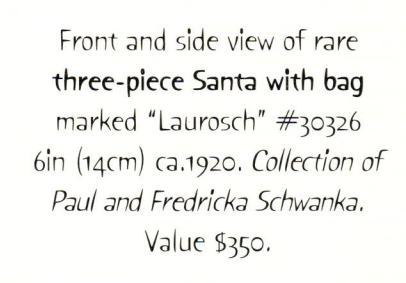

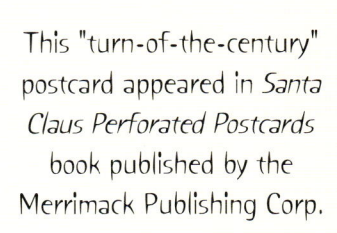

109

Right: **Santa with reindeer**
5in (11-½cm) ca.1940.
Value $150

Below: Master dies used to make the **Santa with Reindeer** mold. *Collection of the American Chocolate Mould Co.*

110

Master dies used to make the **Santa with Reindeer** mold. *Collection of the American Chocolate Mould Co.*

111

Right: **Santa with bag of toys** marked "Anton Reiche" #26313 — 7in (16-½cm) ca.1910. *Mold from the collection of Moni Marceau and Chalkware by Moni Marceau.* Value $395

Bottom left: **Santa with switch** marked "Heris" #167 — 5-½in (13cm) ca.1920. Value $175

Bottom right: **Santa with shoulder bag** marked "Anton Reiche" 5in (11-½cm) ca.1900. Value $225

112

Santa on skis marked "Walters"
#8091 — 7in (17cm) ca.1920.
Collection of Moni Marceau.
Value $375

Above: **Santa driving car** #1026 — 6in (14cm) ca.1940.
Value $195

Left: **Santa riding motorcycle** marked "Vormenfabriek"
#15291 — 5in (11-½cm) ca.1950.
Value $125

113

Angel riding deer marked "Anton Reiche" #24450 6in (14cm) ca.1920. *Collection of Moni Marceau.* Value $400

This "turn-of-the-century" postcard appeared in *Santa Claus Perforated Postcards* book published by the Merrimack Publishing Corp.

Santa riding donkey marked "Letang" #3727
7-½in (18cm) ca.1920.
Value $150

Santa riding donkey marked "Heris" #170
6in (14cm) ca.1920.
Value $150

Santa pulling sled with help from an angel marked
"Hornlein" #1032 — 7-¾in (119cm) ca.1940.
Collection of Paul and Fredricka Schwanka.
Value $300

115

Right: Santa with switch and two children marked "Anton Reiche" #26313 — 8in (19cm) ca.1920. Mold from collection of Moni Marceau and Chalkware by Moni Marceau. Value $375

Bottom left: Santa with puppet marked "Walters" 8-½in (20-½cm) ca.1920. Value $175

Bottom right: Smaller version of the Santa with puppet marked "Walters" 4in (9cm) ca.1920. Notice the two different styles of flanges (the way the mold is trimmed) by the same mold maker. Value $150

Hinged Santa holding airplane marked "Walters" 8-½in (20-½cm) ca.1920. Value $195

Below: Page from the Anton Reiche catalog. ca.1920

Above: **Santa with a satchel full of apples** marked "Jaburg" #24 — 9in (22cm) ca.1910.
Value $295

Right: **Santa with bag** 9-½in (23cm) ca.1920.
Value $150

118

This "turn-of-the-century" postcard appeared in *Santa Claus Perforated Postcards* book published by the Merrimack Publishing Corp.

Extremely Rare Window Display Santa with toys marked "Anton Reiche" #14191 — 20in (48cm) ca.1910. *Collection of Rudi and Isabelle Nuyens.* Value $6,000

119

Left: **Jolly Santa** marked "Jaburg" #44 7-½in (18cm) ca.1910. Value $150

Below left: **Christmas tree** marked "Weygandt" #25215 — 6in (14cm) ca.1910. Value $150
below right: Santa marked "Anton Reiche" #21123 5in (11-½cm) ca.1920. Value $195

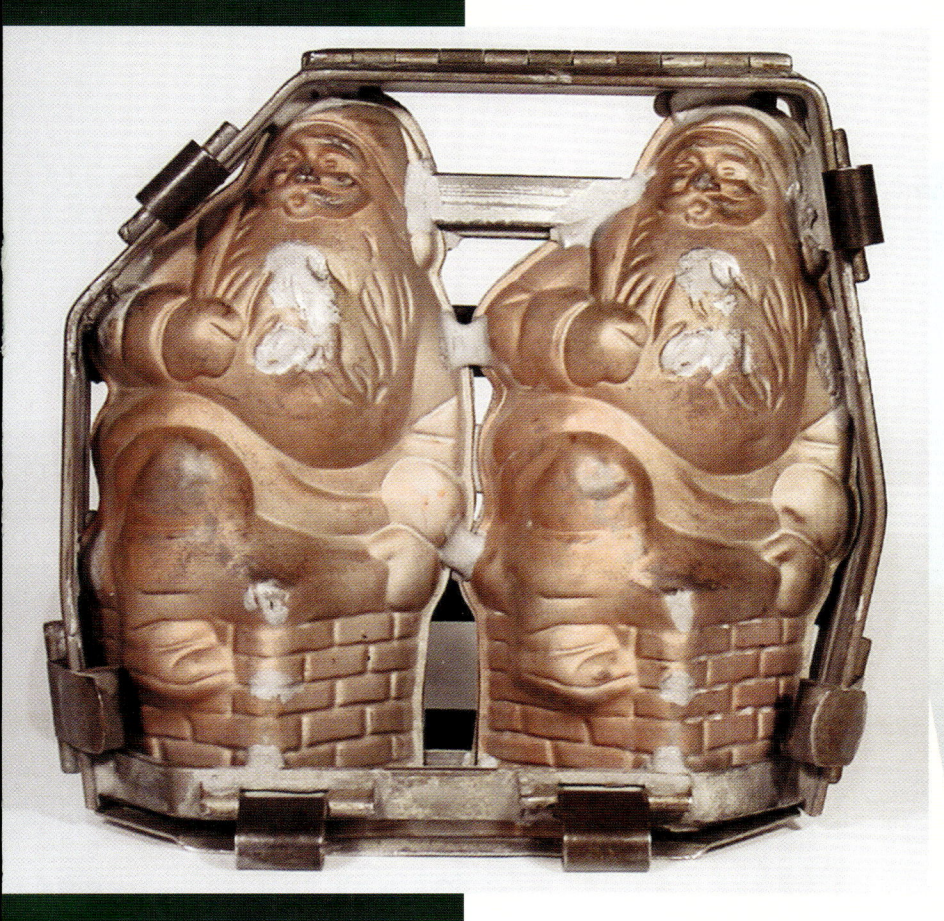

Above: **Hinged Santas coming out of chimney** marked "Weygandt"
7in (16-½cm) ca.1920.
Value $195

Molded chocolate Santa coming out of chimney-courtesy of Rex Morgen at Morgen Chocolate.

Little St. Nick riding a horse marked "Anton Reiche" #29014
4in (9cm) ca.1920.
Value $150

121

Top left: Santa pulling ear of bad boy marked "Heris" #180 6-½in (15-½cm) ca.1920. Value $275

Top right: Exhausted Santa #5527 5in (11-½cm) ca.1920. Collection of Moni Marceau. Value $275

This "turn-of-the-century" postcard appeared in *Santa Claus Perforated Postcards* book published by the Merrimack Publishing Corp.

122

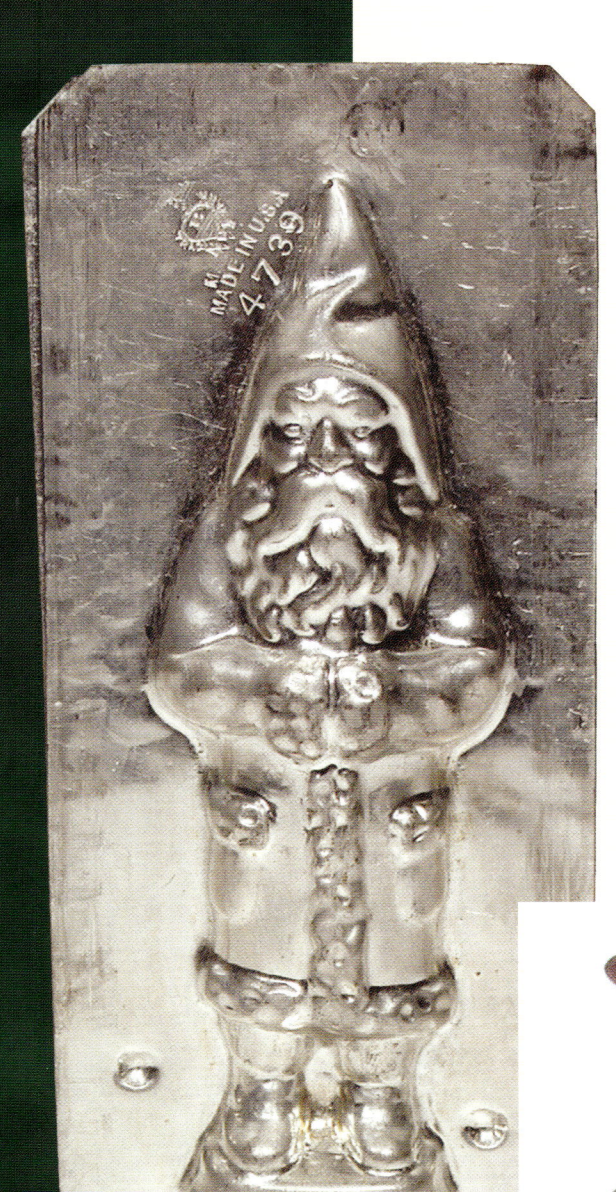

Left: Santa with hands in muff marked "Eppelsheimer" #4739 6-½in (15-½cm) ca.1920.
Value $150

Below: Santa holding lantern
8in (19cm) ca.1910. *Molded chocolate Santa with lantern-courtesy of The Chocolate Barn, photo by Christy Nevius.*
Value $175

123

Little Santa holding tree and teddy bear
marked "Anton Reiche" #32826
5in (11-½cm) ca.1920. *Collection of
Paul and Fredricka Schwanka.*
Value $225

Santa's helper marked
"Anton Reiche"
6in (14cm) ca.1920.
Value $175

Front and back view of
Window Display Santa marked
"Hornlein" #1109
16in (38cm) ca.1950.
Value $500

125

Above: **Postcard mold depicting children with Christmas toys** marked "Anton Reiche" #522 — 7in (16-½cm) ca.1910.
Collection of Moni Marceau.
Value $375

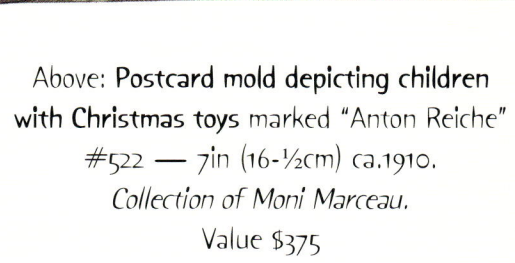

Right: **Strange Santa with face shown on front and back** halves of mold #1473 7in (16-½cm) ca.1940. *Collection of Paul and Fredricka Schwanka.*
Value $250

126

Page from the Anton Reiche catalog, ca.1920

Above: **Santa with bag** 7in (16-½cm) ca.1920.
Value $150

Above right: **Santa with small purse** marked "Laurosch" 4-¾in (11cm) ca.1930.
Value $175

Right: **Little Santa** marked "Hornlein" #165 — 3-½in (7-½cm) ca.1930. Chocolate Santa made with candy melts.
Value $150

Santa with hands in muff
5in (11-½cm) ca.1940.
Value $125

Front and back view of **Three Santas and an angel riding a sled**
6in (14cm) ca.1920.
Value $450

129

Right: **Flat mold of Santas holding axes** marked "Vormenfabriek" 13in (31cm) ca.1950. Value $95

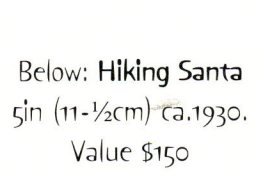

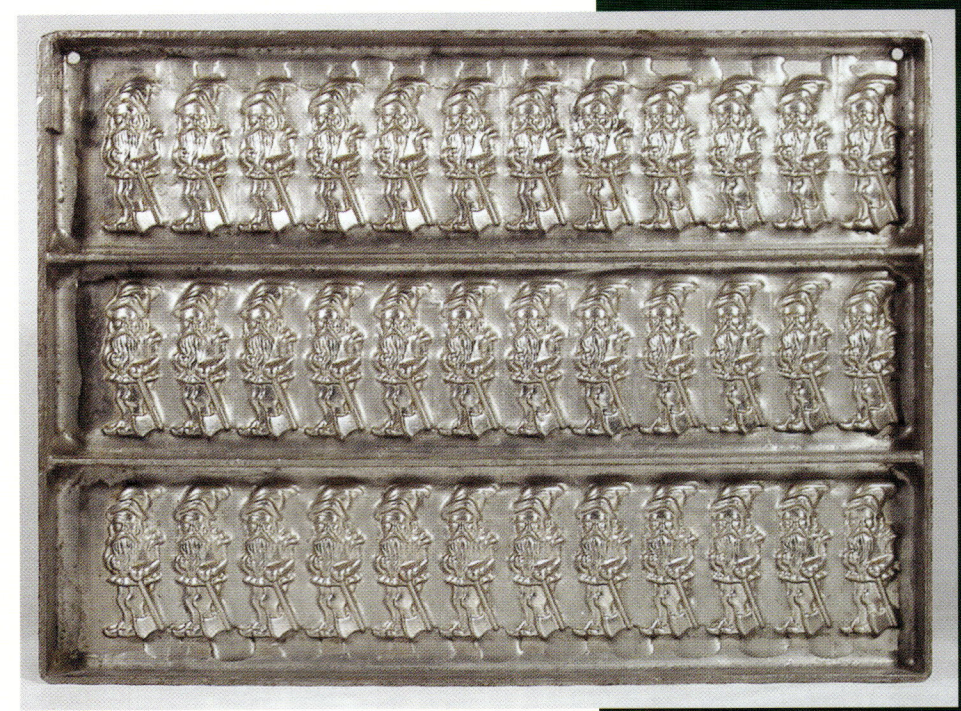

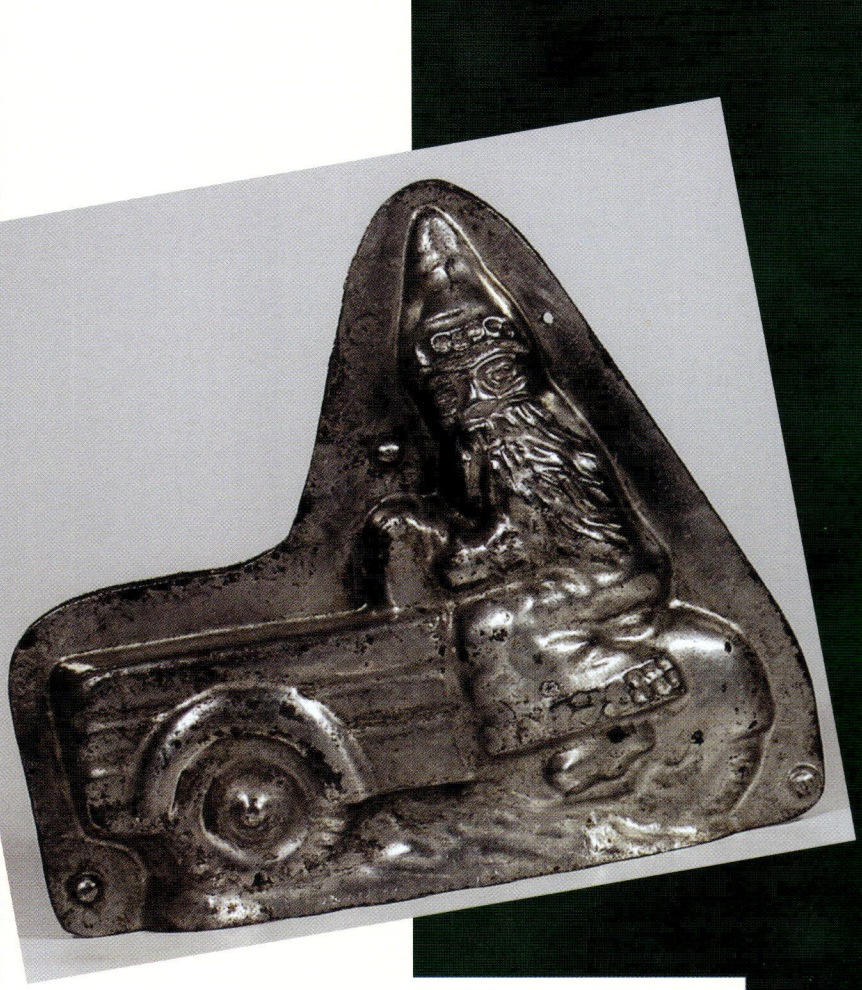

Below: **Hiking Santa** 5in (11-½cm) ca.1930. Value $150

Santa driving cargo hauler 6-½in (15cm) ca.1930. Value $150

130

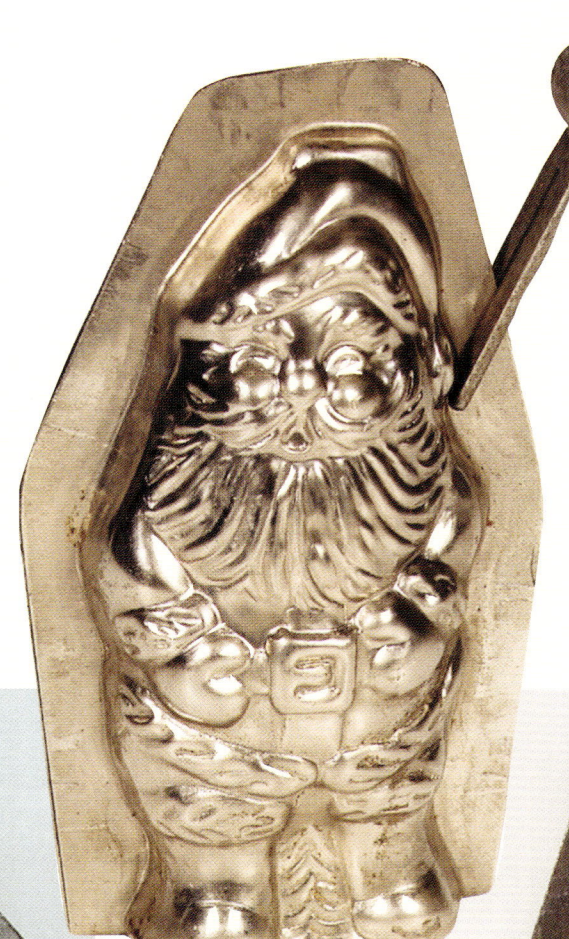

Jolly Santa
5in (11-½cm) ca.1950.
Value $75

Below: **Santa with hands in sleeves** marked "Riecke" #4012 — 7in (16-½cm) ca.1920.
Value $175

Below: **French Santa** marked "Letang" #2039 7-½in (18cm) ca.1920.
Value $150

131

Above: **Hinged Santa with bag of apples** 9in (22cm) ca.1910.
Value $195

Above right: **Santa with bag** #15554 5in (11-½cm) ca.1950.
Value $125

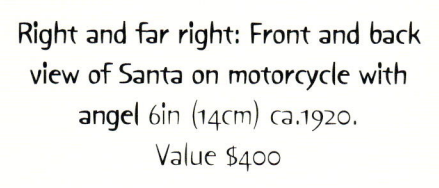

Right and far right: Front and back view of **Santa on motorcycle with angel** 6in (14cm) ca.1920.
Value $400

132

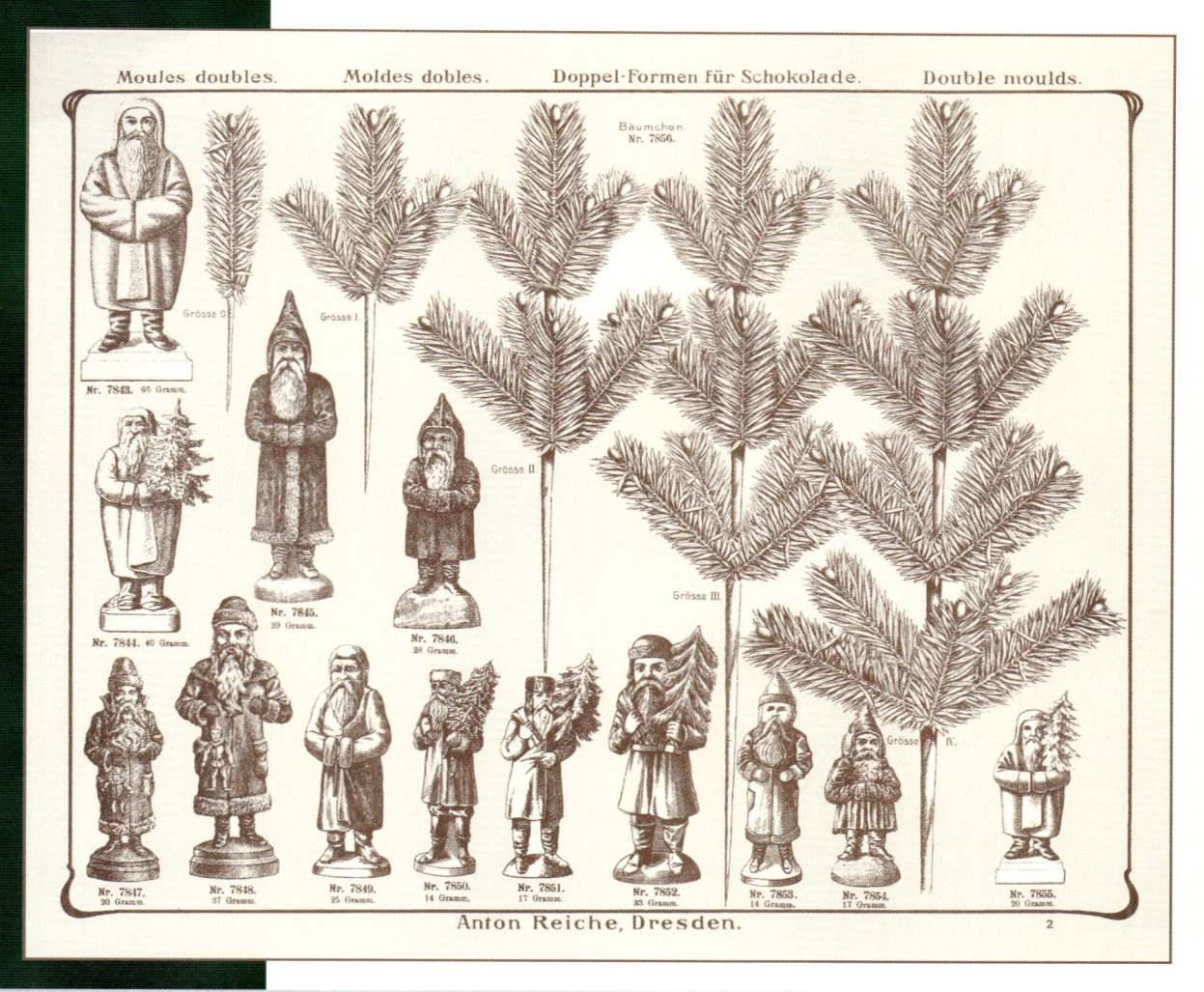

Above: Page from the Anton Reiche catalog, ca.1920

133

Above: Rare **St. Nick mold with plug in the top** marked "Anton Reiche" #15540 8-½in (20cm) ca.1910.
Value $275

St. Nick's head
5-½in (13cm) ca.1920.
Value $125

Above: **St. Nick with children** marked "Anton Reiche" #15540 8in (19cm) ca.1910.
*Note-these are exactly the same mold numbers but one has the plug on top.
Value $225

Three sizes of St. Nick-*Left*
4in (9cm) ca.1910.
Value $95
Center marked "Anton Reiche"
6-½in (15-½cm) ca.1910.
Value $150
Right marked "Letang"
3in (6-½cm) ca.1910.
Value $150

Big St. Nick with children in tub #10388
12-½in (30cm) ca.1900.
Value $250

Tall St. Nick marked "Vormenfabriek" #15441
16in (38cm) ca.1950.
Value $150

135

~Miscellaneous~

Vehicles for Transportation

Motorcycle marked "Dehaeck" #16232 7in (16-½cm) ca.1930. Value $95
Airplane 7in (16-½cm) ca.1940. Value $75
Train marked "Anton Reiche" #9954 5in (11-½cm) ca.1920. Value $175
Army truck marked "Anton Reiche" #16738 4-½in (10-½cm) ca.1940. Value $95

Hot air balloon marked "Sommet" 12in (29cm) ca.1910. Value $225

Zeppelin #3551 9in (21-½cm) ca.1920. Value $250

137

Smoking Items

Big Cigar marked "Anton Reiche" #14036 — 13in (31cm) ca.1930.
Value $150
Santa faced pipe 7in (16-½cm) ca.1920.
Value $150
Pipe 5in (11-½cm) ca.1930.
Value $65
Large flat mold of cigars 10in (24cm) ca.1920.
Value $125
Small flat mold of cigars marked "Eppelsheimer" 8in (19cm) ca.1910.
Value $75

Shoes

Big Santa boot 8in (19cm)
ca.1920.
Value $75
Smaller work boot
5in (11-½cm) ca.1920.
Value $55
Large wooden clog 6in (14cm)
ca.1910.
Value $45
Small clog 3in (6-½cm)
ca.1910.
Value $40

Guns

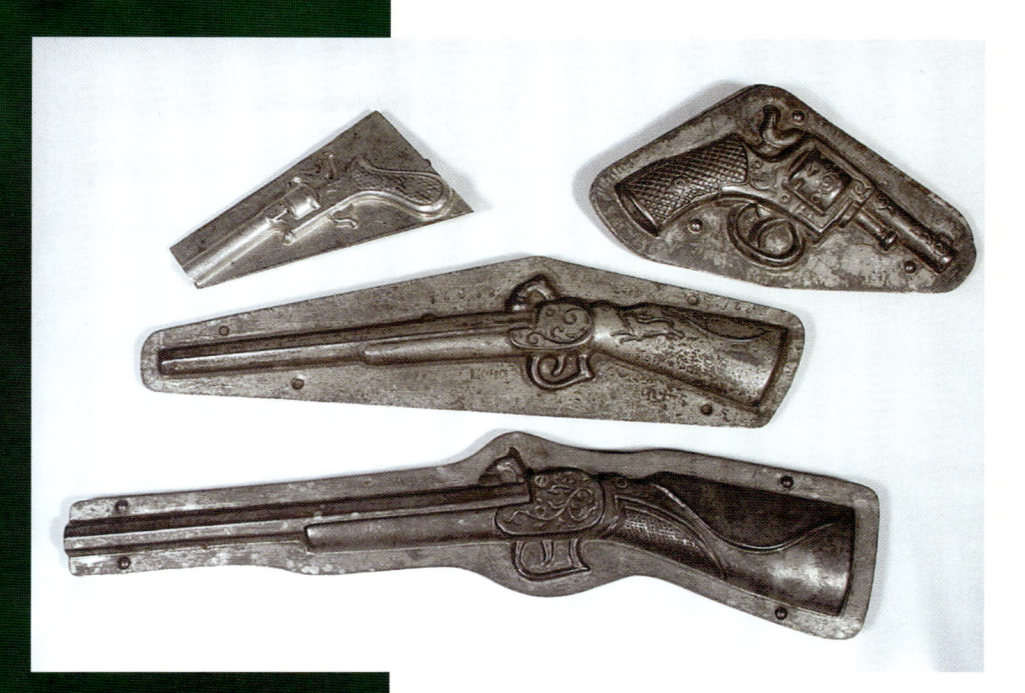

Largest Rifle marked
"Anton Reiche" #10014
15in (35cm) ca.1910.
Value $175
Rifle marked "Riecke"
12-½in (30cm) ca.1910.
Value $150
Revolver marked "Anton Reiche"
#9942 — 8in (19cm) ca.1910.
Value $95
Small revolver 5in (11-½cm)
ca.1920.
Value $75

Instruments

Violin marked "Anton Reiche" #14916
8in (19cm) ca.1910.
Value $150
Mandolin 7-½in (18cm) ca.1930.
Value $75
Large horn marked "Anton Reiche" #10174
6in (14cm) ca.1910.
Value $75
Small horn marked "Anton Reiche" #10174
4in (9cm) ca.1910.
Value $50

*Note –both horns have the same number although they are different in size.

Additional Information

American Chocolate Mould Company

American Chocolate Mould Company began in 1910 as a manufacturer of metal molds and was one of the leading metal mold manufacturers located in Manhattan from 1912 to 1971. The Friedwald family has run the company since it began. American Chocolate Mould Company purchased Eppelsheimer mold company and currently represents B.V. Vormenfabriek Tilburg. Today American Chocolate Mould Company is the largest manufacturer of plastic molds for the chocolate and confectionery industry. They also do modeling work for chocolate molds and act as a service organization to the confectionery industry. Metal chocolate molds made from the original hand-carved iron dies, dating from 1920, are being manufactured and are available for purchase from the website: *www.americanchocolatemould.com*.

New Santa mold stamped from original dies available from the American Chocolate Mould Co.

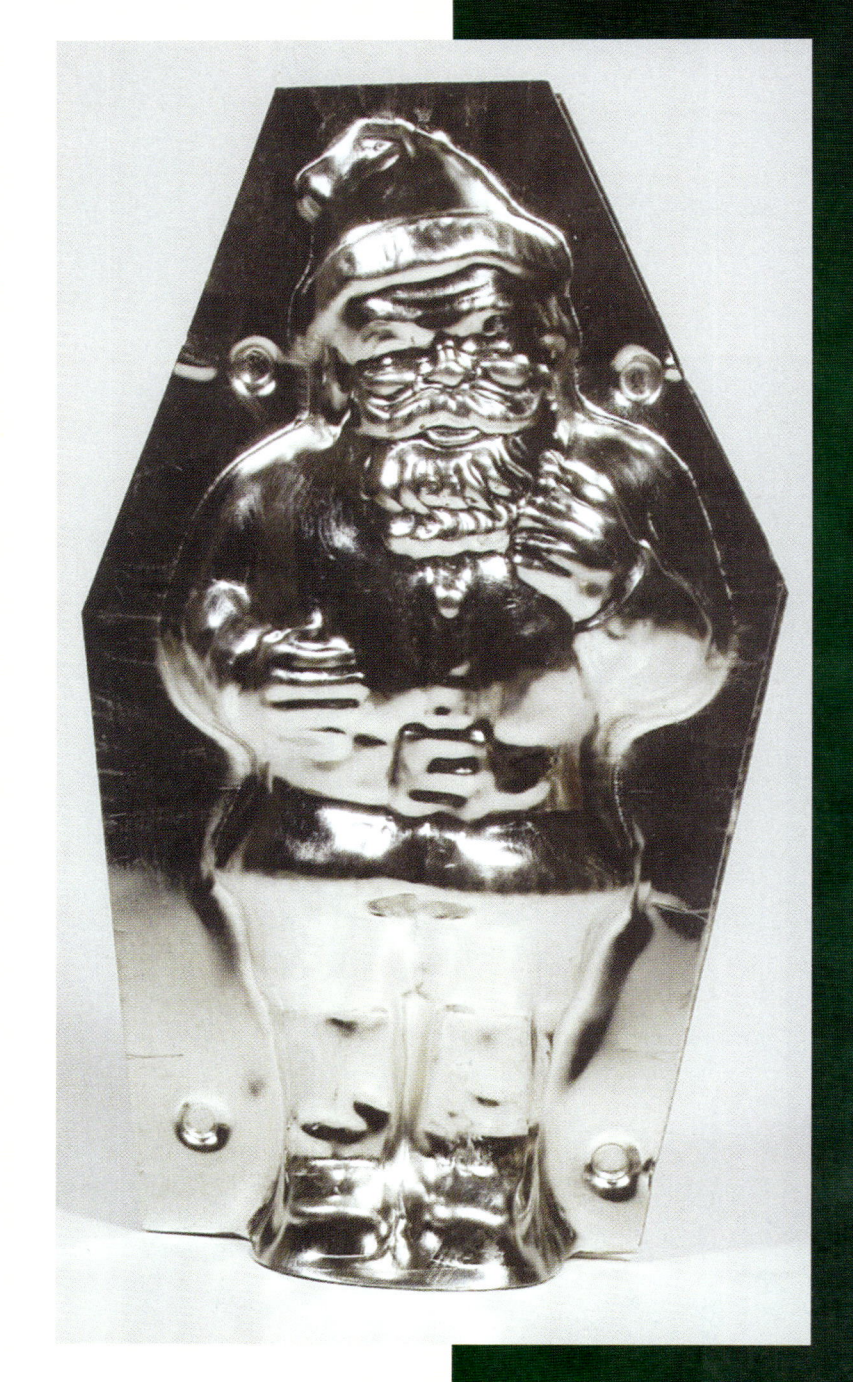

Above: Page from an old American Chocolate Mould catalog shown with similar molds.

Right: New **bunny** mold stamped from original dies available from the American Chocolate Mould Co. Chocolate bunny made with "Wilton candy melts" by author and children.

141

The Chocolate Barn

The Chocolate Barn owned and operated by Lucinda Gregory is located in Vermont. Lucinda currently uses over 500 antique chocolate molds to form figures made of Swiss chocolate. Lucinda also has over 200 antique chocolate molds available for purchase.

Sitting teddy bear marked "Anton Reiche" #24015 6in (14cm) ca.1920. *Molded chocolate bear courtesy of The Chocolate Barn, photo by Christy Nevius.* Value $400

Inside view of The Chocolate Barn, *photo by Christy Nevius.*

142

Morgen Chocolate

Morgen Chocolate is located in Dallas, Texas. The company uses both metal and plastic molds. They also design new molds. The owner, Rex Morgen apprenticed under a European Master Chocolatier. He continues the tradition of using the highest quality chocolate for molding. For more information visit *MorgenChocolate.com*.

Molded chocolate of the **Big standing teddy bear** - *Courtesy of Morgen Chocolate.*

Moni Marceau

Casting Chalkware from Antique Chocolate Molds is Moni Marceau's way of sharing the art and preserving the skill of her predecessors. Her tools are her brushes and original antique chocolate molds. Moni combines history and art by recreating Santas and other forms for her friends and family. Moni's finely painted artifacts are available at shows and she can be commissioned to cast pieces from antique molds. Where possible, the molds genealogy will be traced based upon her extensive and continuing research into the history of the molds and their makers. Contact Moni at: *www.monisfolkart.com*.

Boy with toy horse marked "Anton Reiche" #7531 — 6in (14cm) ca.1920
Girl with doll marked "Anton Reiche" #7532 — 6in (14cm) ca.1920.
Molds and Chalkware courtesy of Moni Marceau.
Value $350 for the pair

Children at candy store window, ca.1940.